THE CATHOLIC BIBLICAL QUARTERLY MONOGRAPH SERIES

19

THE OLD GREEK TRANSLATION OF DANIEL 7–12

by

Sharon Pace Jeansonne

THE OLD GREEK TRANSLATION
OF DANIEL 7–12

by
Sharon Pace Jeansonne

PICKWICK *Publications*
An imprint of *Wipf and Stock Publishers*

Pickwick Publications
An imprint of Wipf and Stock Publishers
199 W 8th Ave, Suite 3
Eugene, OR 97401

The Old Greek Translation of Daniel 7–12
By Jeansonne, Sharon Pace
Copyright © 1988 The Catholic Biblical Association of America All rights reserved.
Softcover ISBN-13: 978-1-6667-8637-8
Hardcover ISBN-13: 978-1-6667-8638-5
eBook ISBN-13: 978-1-6667-8639-2
Publication date 7/10/2023
Previously published by The Catholic Biblical Association of America, 1988

This edition is a scanned facsimile of the original edition published in 1988.

TO MY TEACHER
EUGENE ULRICH

והמשכלים יזהרו כזהר הרקיע

TABLE OF CONTENTS

ACKNOWLEDGMENTS

The closure of this study would not be complete without an expression of my appreciation to my mentor, Eugene Ulrich, under whose guidance I was introduced to textual criticism and to the study of the texts of Daniel. Prof. Ulrich read an earlier form of this work which was submitted as my dissertation, and this study has immensely benefitted from his critique. I am also indebted to Josephine Massyngbaerde Ford, James Walsh, and Joseph Blenkinsopp, who served on my dissertation committee and offered many insightful suggestions. In the summer of 1985 a National Endowment for the Humanities grant enabled me to have the privilege of studying with Louis Feldman who opened up new avenues of exploration into the Greek translations of Daniel. Moreover, I thank Robert Karris and the two anonymous readers of my manuscript for their careful reading and suggestions for revisions. The task of typing this manuscript was made infinitely more manageable by the generous gift of time by Richard Edwards, who designed the program for my computer to print Hebrew and Greek letters. There are many friends who helped me at the various stages of the project and I thank my husband, Glen Jeansonne, who gave me much assistance and encouragement in the final stages of this work.

ABBREVIATIONS AND SIGLA

G	The Old Greek Text
H	The (oldest recoverable) Semitic Text
LXX	Septuagint
M, MT	The Masoretic Text
OG	Old Greek
Q	The Qumran Text
SP	The Samaritan Pentateuch
Syh	The Syro-Hexapla
α′	The text of Aquila
θ′	The text of Theodotion
ο′	The Septuagint Text of Origen
σ′	The text of Symmachus
88	Manuscript 88
967	Papyrus 967

INTRODUCTION

Purpose

For communities who hold the Scriptures to be normative, the texts serve as a canon or rule of judgment for faith and praxis. In order to determine the intention of particular texts, communities over the centuries have found it necessary to explicate and interpret them in relation to the theological concerns of their own contemporary situation. In the closing centuries of the Second Temple period a prerequisite for Greek-speaking Jewish communities was the translation of their sacred books into Greek from the Hebrew or Aramaic parent text (*Vorlage*). It is axiomatic that translation itself is to a certain extent an interpretation.

This study will investigate the Old Greek (OG) translation of chapters 7–12 of Daniel which preserves the earliest written interpretation of what the text meant for a member of the Jewish community of the Diaspora. The investigation is limited to the translator responsible for chapters 7–12 since the nature of the more free translation in chapters 1–6 requires either that different translators be posited for the two sections, or that the *Vorlage* of the OG was more divergent from our *textus receptus* in chapters 1–6 than in chapters 7–12.[1] Moreover, the form and content of chapters 7–12, namely, the first person accounts of the visions which date from the time of Antiochus Epiphanes, differ considerably from chapters 1–6 and thereby allow for a separate consideration. The primary purpose of this investigation is to determine whether differences between the OG translation and the Hebrew/Aramaic parent text of Daniel 7–12 are due to intentional theological *Tendenz*, as has been predominantly proposed in the past, or to errors or the unintentional cross-linguistic mechanics of translation, or to a combination of these reasons. Although studies are limited, previous scholarship on the OG of Daniel reveals a consensus: variants in the o′ text (assumed to equal the OG) are due to a translator who intentionally departed from the Semitic text in accordance with the historical developments and theological interpretations of the day. These studies have made five assumptions about

---

[1] Most notably, Daniel 4–6 contain many variants.

1

the OG which need to be questioned in the light of our knowledge of the history of the text.[2] First, these investigations have failed to distinguish between the original OG, which requires critical reconstruction, and its later version in Origen's Hexapla. Secondly, because of the assumption that the *Vorlage* of the OG was equivalent to the Masoretic text (M), they have not adequately compared the OG to its own *Vorlage*. Thirdly, the overall character of the OG, crucial for providing the proper context in which to judge isolated variants, has never been subjected to statistical analysis or to comprehensive study except for the overview by J. Ziegler in the introduction to the θ′ and o′ texts of Daniel in the Göttingen edition.[3] Fourthly, the possibility that the OG text contains variants which are prompted by mechanical and linguistic errors, many of which are illumined by recent studies in paleography of the Second Temple period, is not given adequate consideration. Fifthly, the content of the book itself, which provides possibilities for examining variants in view of other usages of the same theme, is often ignored.

Method

This investigation attempts to move beyond past studies on the OG of Daniel by (1) determining more accurately the OG itself as opposed to subsequent Greek developments, (2) investigating the possible *Vorlage* of the OG, (3) delineating the character of the OG translation of Daniel 7-12 as a whole, (4) noting the typical errors of the OG, and (5) examining true variants in the light of other similar passages which provide a context for comparison and evaluation whenever they are available.

An understanding of the history of the text and the translations and recensions of other biblical books enables us to posit the development of the same for Daniel, which is delineated in Chapter I below. Past investigations have failed to distinguish between the original OG and the partially mixed textual witnesses to the OG in Origen's attempt to restore the Septuagint, and have not left room for the possibility that the OG *Vorlage* was other than the Hebrew and Aramaic of M; rather, the *Vorlage* was assumed to be identical to M. Recent advances in textual studies in the books of Judges, Samuel–Kings, Isaiah, Jeremiah, and Job have advanced our understanding of the relationship between the OG translation and its *Vorlage*. The Qumran scrolls sometimes show that the Greek translators used a text distinct from the *textus receptus*. Moreover, manuscript evidence from 4QDan[a,b,c] and Papyrus 967 (967) assist in more accurately determining the OG *Vorlage* and

---

[2] For discussion of these works, see below, Chapter I.

[3] J. Ziegler, ed. *Susanna, Daniel, Bel et Draco* (Septuaginta Vetus Testamentum Graecum 16/2; Göttingen: Vandenhoeck and Ruprecht, 1954).

the OG itself. It is sometimes possible to show that a Greek reading which earlier would have been categorized as a "variant" introduced by the translator, since it disagreed with M, is now seen to be an accurate translation of an alternate *Vorlage*. The present study will utilize all the extant Qumran texts and 967 readings which illumine the character of the OG text as a whole and its relationship to θ' and M. We proceed as follows:

Chapter I lists available texts and editions whence the data for the Hebrew and Greek versions of Daniel are drawn. It will include a discussion of the problematic nature of the witnesses to the OG. Secondly, an operating hypothesis of the history and stratigraphy of the book of Daniel is offered, including its basis in past studies on the text and subsequent translation and recensions of the Hebrew Bible in general, the actual stages of development, Hebrew scribal copying, and its translation and recensions in Greek. Thirdly, we will survey selected important past studies on the OG of Daniel, briefly assessing their overall contributions and limitations.

Chapter II delineates the typical procedures of the OG translation by investigating one sample continuous passage as well as sample test cases. The continuous passage provides data for a statistical sample of the OG translational procedure, as well as the θ' text's recension of that translation. Our familiarity with the typical characteristics of the OG puts us in a better position to assess the reasons why variants occur and to determine more accurately the true OG reading when the manuscript evidence suggests something other than the o' reading in difficult or suspicious cases. The sample test cases illustrate the OG translator's use of lexical choices, grammatical procedure, and general approach to the translation of the Semitic text.

Chapter III studies examples of errors which the OG made due to misreadings of the *Vorlage* or to the use of a *Vorlage* which contained scribal errors. We look at representative readings of substitution of individual letters, omissions of individual letters and words, metatheses and confused word and sentence division. By noting that mechanical errors occur not infrequently we are assured that it is sound judgment to investigate the possibility that variants which *prima facie* appear to come from an intentional change might actually be due to simple errors.

Chapter IV lists inner Greek variants which cannot be explained simply by either a misreading or misunderstanding of the *Vorlage* and which come from secondary errors, namely, changes which come not from the OG translator but from later scribes. These variants are subdivided into two main categories. First, we discuss secondary errors which are not indicative of any theological changes, and are clearly caused by mechanical errors from the hands of later Greek scribes who misunderstood the original OG text. Included are doublets, additions, omissions, and misunderstood letters. Secondly, we investigate secondary errors and changes which possibly are illustrative of distinct theological or historical significance. In the course of the investigation of these readings, we present other critics' claims that they are actually OG variants, followed by our reasons for categorizing these variants as secondary errors. The content of these readings include the Ancient of Days (Dan 7:13), the dating of Cyrus's tenure (Dan 10:1), the attitude toward the Ptolemies (Dan 11:25), and those who rise from the earth (Dan 12:2).

Chapter V examines the variants which came, not from later developments, but from the OG translator. The concern here will be to determine whether the changes which occurred at the level of the OG translator were intentional or unintentional.

Some of these variants occur in passages which have parallels elsewhere in the book of Daniel; others occur in passages dealing with topics which would be prime candidates for theological elaboration or embellishment, if such had indeed been the practice of the translator. Such topics include the Son of Man, the four kingdoms, the time of the end, and resurrection. We will compare all of these references to see whether similar variations occur. If, for example, a variant calculation of the time of the end was intentional, other places in the text which deal with this reference to the time of the end should reflect the same viewpoint. This chapter will not treat references in isolation as has been done in scholarly works since the time of the first major study of the OG by A. Bludau,[4] but will view them in relation to other passages by the same OG translator which throw light on the context of the variants under consideration.

Chapter VI reviews the conclusions of the previous chapters and presents overall conclusions about the OG text of Daniel 7–12. Having developed the proper understanding of the history and stratigraphy of the OG text of Daniel, the approach of the translator to the *Vorlage,* and having delineated the kinds of variants and the reasons which give rise to them, we will be on solid ground to assess the nature of this translation.

---

[4] A. Bludau, "Die alexandrinische Uebersetzung des Buches Daniel und ihr Verhältniss zum massorethischen Text," *Bib S* (F) II/2-3 (1897) v–218.

I

BACKGROUND TO THE STUDY OF THE OLD GREEK OF DANIEL: TEXTS AND EDITIONS, HISTORY AND STRATIGRAPHY, AND PREVIOUS STUDIES

Introduction

In order to begin a text-critical investigation of the OG of Daniel, familiarity with the manuscripts and editions which provide the readings of the OG, θ', and M is required. The number of manuscripts available and their condition and reliability help to determine the text critic's judgment concerning the preferred reading of an original text or its translation. In this chapter we include a listing of texts and editions of Daniel followed by a working hypothesis for the history and stratigraphy of the text of Daniel, based upon the manuscript evidence for Daniel as well as our knowledge of the history and stratigraphy of other books of the Hebrew Scriptures. This hypothesis forms the basis of the following chapters when judgments are made about the original OG, its probable *Vorlage,* and the Theodotionic revisions, as well as when the reliability of the Masoretic Text's witness to the original Hebrew is determined. This background concerning the available manuscripts and history and stratigraphy of the text of Daniel equips us to present a brief summary and critique of the strengths and limitations of the more important previous studies on the OG of Daniel.

Texts and Editions

The following texts are used in this study:

Hebrew and Aramaic Witnesses

The Hebrew and Aramaic text of Daniel used as customary standard is that of *Biblia Hebraica Stuttgartensia* edited by W. Baumgartner which is based upon the Leningrad Codex B 19A dated to 1009 or 1008 C.E. G. Weil describes its composition:

> The great Masoretic manuscripts, such as L, were composed by transcribing texts from individual manuscripts of different parts of the Bible. The manuscripts were themselves copied from manuscripts which earlier teachers had prepared for the use of their students by adding marginal notes derived from a variety of commentaries, often representing rival schools of scribes and Masoretes.[1]

Included in the *BHS* apparatus for Dan M are the fragmentary Hebrew/ Aramaic manuscript evidence from the Cairo geniza and the Masoretic variants collected by B. Kennicott and J. B. de Rossi.

In addition to the Masoretic text of Daniel there are fragmentary manuscripts from Qumran: 1QDan[a,b], 4QDan[a,b,c] and 6QDan.[2] Fragments from caves 1 and 6 show little variation from the text preserved in M, and their most interesting contribution for the study of the text of Daniel is that in both 1QDan[a] and M, the Aramaic section begins at 2:4b.[3] Otherwise, the variants present in 1QDan[a,b] and 6QDan are not particularly striking, since no changes in meaning are apparent. Typical orthographic variants are found, as well as slight variation of forms. For example, in Dan 10:11

---

[1] G. Weil, Prolegomena to *BHS* (ed. K. Elliger and W. Rudolph; Stuttgart: Deutsche Bibelstiftung, 1977) xiv.

[2] 1QDan[a,b] are found in D. Barthélemy and J. T. Milik, *Qumran Cave I* (DJD 1; Oxford: Clarendon, 1955) 150–52. Cf. J. C. Trever, "Completion of the Publication of Some Fragments from Qumran Cave I," *RevQ* 5 (1964–66) 323–44. Information on 4QDan[a,b,c] is found below and in note 4. 6QDan is found in M. Baillet, J. T. Milik, and R. de Vaux, *Les 'Petites Grottes' de Qumran* (DJD 3; Oxford: Clarendon, 1962) 114–16. 1QDan[a] contains 1:10–17 and 2:2–6; 1QDan[b] contains 3:22–30. Both 1QDan[a] and 1QDan[b] date from the Herodian period. 6QDan contains 8:16–17 (?), 8:20–21 (?), 10:8–16, 11:33–36, 38, dated to ca. 50 C.E. There are two further fragmentary manuscripts of Daniel: 4QDan[d] with 13 small, nearly illegible fragments and 4QDan[e] with 5 tiny fragments from Daniel 9.

[3] Cf. the statement of A. Di Lella, "instead of the MT gloss *'ărāmît*, 'Aramaic,' 1QDan[a] leaves a space between the Hebrew and Aramaic text," in *The Book of Daniel* (AB 23; Garden City: Doubleday, 1978) 73. The case should be stated more precisely. The right half of the column with the lines containing 2:2–6 is preserved, while the left half has been lost. 2:4b begins on a new line with indentation, thus with a space before the Aramaic section. But 2:4a is mostly off the leather; there is space for ארמית to have been included at the end of the line before the new line with 2:4b. Thus, though the gloss is not preserved in 1QDan[a], we cannot state or presume that it was omitted.

The Book of Daniel was written by both Di Lella and L. Hartman. Di Lella (*The Book of Daniel,* vii) explains, "Before his death, Hartman completed the translation, text-critical apparatus, and explanatory notes of all twelve chapters of the Book of Daniel as well as the commentary on chapters 1–9." Di Lella wrote the commentary on Daniel 10–12 and the introduction. The authors are appropriately distinguished in this work.

6QDan reads ח[מ]מודת (cf. Ezra 8:27) whereas M has חמדות "beloved." In Dan 3:24, 1QDan[b] reads ל[גו and M reads לגוא "to the midst." In Dan 3:27, 1QDan[b] reads ושרבל[ן]יהון whereas M has וסרבליהון "and their mantles." Two non-orthographic variants are as follows. In Dan 10:13 6QDan has מ[ן]לכות פרס "the kingdom of Persia" whereas M reads מלכי פרס "the kings of Persia," and in Dan 10:15 6QDan has אפי "my face/nose" whereas M reads פני "my face." Yet even these variants do not indicate any significant changes of meaning.

4QDan[a,b,c] is presently being prepared for preliminary publication by E. Ulrich, and his final publication will appear in DJD.[4] Ulrich dates 4QDan[a] to the middle of the first century B.C.E., and F. M. Cross dates 4QDan[b] to 20–50 C.E. and 4QDan[c] to 100–50 B.C.E.[5] Ulrich lists the contents of 4QDan as follows: 4QDan[a]: 1:16–20; 2:9–11, 19–49; 3:1–2; 4:29–30; 5:5–7, 12–14, 16–19; 7:5–6, 25–28; 8:1–5; 10:16–20; 11:13–16. 4QDan[b]: 5:10–11, 14–16, 19–22; 6:8–22, 27–29; 7:1–6, 26–28; 8:1–8; 13–16. 4QDan[c]: 10:5–9, 11–16, 21; 11:1–2, 13–17; 11:25–29.[6] These readings have been utilized in the gathering of data for this work, and we have included all relevant variants for our discussion of the OG of Daniel. Most 4QDan readings agree with M, although there are a few significant variants and several orthographic variants. These are discussed throughout the following chapters, although we call attention to the following examples at present: In Dan 8:3, M has קרנים והקרנים "horns, and the horns," whereas both 4QDan[a] and Dan[b] read (ut vid.) קרנים קרנים [והקרנים] "sets of horns, and the horns." In Dan 8:4 M has ימה וצפונה "westward and northward," where 4QDan[a] reads י[מ]ה ומזרחה צפונה "westward and eastward, northward." In Dan 8:5 M has על פני "upon the face" whereas 4QDan[a] reads אל פני "toward the face." In Dan 8:3 M has איל אחד "one ram," whereas 4QDan[a] reads איל אחד גד[ול and 4QDan[b] reads איל אחד] גדול "one great ram." These variants point out that the history of the text of Daniel is more complex than is often assumed and caution us that M, albeit the main witness, fully preserved as it is, is not the only text of Daniel but one witness among several to the text of Daniel.

---

[4] E. Ulrich, "Daniel Manuscripts from Qumran. Part 1: A Preliminary Edition of 4QDan[a]," *BASOR* 268 (1987) 17–37. This writer is grateful to Prof. Ulrich who has made available the text of this article before publication. Moreover, this writer is grateful to Profs. Cross and Ulrich for their permission to use the Dan Q photographs and to consult the original fragments in Jerusalem.

[5] F. M. Cross, "Editing the Manuscript Fragments from Qumran: Cave 4 of Qumran (4Q)," *BA* 19 (1956) 86; "The Development of the Jewish Scripts," *The Bible in the Ancient Near East* (ed. G. E. Wright; Garden City: Doubleday, 1961) 139 line 6; 149 line 2. "Le travail d'édition des fragments manuscrits de Qumran," *RB* 63 (1956) 58.

[6] The preliminary edition of 4QDan[b] and 4QDan[c] by Ulrich will also appear in *BASOR*.

Besides these Hebrew and Aramaic texts there are several additional sources of Hebrew quotations and allusions, including 4QpsDan, 4QFlor, and the numerous references in the midrashim and Talmud to Daniel. 4QpsDan does not preserve any direct quotations, and 4QFlor has two brief quotations or allusions from Dan 11:32 and 12:10.[7] We note, for example, that 4QFlor reads ויצטרפו for the M reading ויצרפו "and they shall be refined" of Dan 12:10.[8] The Mekilta alone has over twenty-five references to the biblical text and to the person Daniel.[9] Additional midrashic references are found in *Pirqe R. El., Mid. Pss., Cant. Rab., 'Abot R. Nat.,* and *Pesiq. R.*[10] The Talmud contains over one-hundred thirty citations to the biblical text, and the person Daniel is referred to in eleven tractates.[11]

Witnesses to the Old Greek of Daniel

The OG text, which we define as the oldest recoverable form of the first translation into Greek of the Hebrew/Aramaic text of Daniel, can only be reconstructed. This reconstruction is hampered by the paucity of manuscript evidence and few secondary witnesses. The data include the hexaplaric evidence from manuscript 88 (88), the Syro-Hexapla (Syh), Papyrus 967 (967), patristic quotations, and many readings of θ′ wherein θ′ actually preserves the OG. The manuscript evidence for θ′, on the other hand, is not nearly as meager. Several uncial and minuscule manuscripts are extant, as well as many patristic quotations.[12]

The Hexapla

Since our main witnesses for the OG, 88, and Syh, come from the Hexapla of Origen, a few remarks are in order concerning this monumental

[7] See J. M. Allegro, *Qumran Cave 4: 1 (4Q 158–4Q 186)* (DJD 5; Oxford: Clarendon, 1968) 54, and pl. XIX, frg. 3. Cf. J. Strugnell, "Notes en marge du vol. v des 'Discoveries in the Judaean Desert of Jordan,'" *RevQ* 7 (1970) 177, 220–37.

[8] A. Mertens, *Das Buch Daniel im Lichte der Texte vom Toten Meer* (SBM 12; Würzburg: Echter; Stuttgart: Katholisches Bibelwerk, 1971) 29. Mertens explains "Statt ויצטרפו hat MT יצרפו [but read ויצרפו], doch findet sich in palästinensischen Handschriften auch die Form יתצרפו, freilich ohne metathesis und Umwandlung des ח."

[9] J. Lauterbach, *Mekilta de-Rabbi Ishmael* (3 vols.; Philadelphia: Jewish Publication Society, 1935), 3. 239, 254. The rabbinic references do not provide any variants of interest for a text-critical study of Daniel.

[10] For an excellent introduction to the post-biblical Jewish literature on Daniel see *Encyclopaedia Judaica* 5: 1275–76 and the numerous examples cited therein.

[11] See the list of biblical citations in *The Babylonian Talmud* (London: Soncino, 1952) index vol. 613–14. References to the person Daniel are found in *b. Ber.* 7b, 31a; *b. Sanh.* 93a–93b, 98b; *b. Yoma* 69b, 77a; *b. Meg.* 11a–b, 15a; *b. B. Bat.* 4a; *b. 'Abod. Zar.* 3a, 35b–36a.

[12] For a comprehensive listing see Ziegler, *Susanna, Daniel, Bel et Draco,* 28–36.

work. We should not assume that the aims of the present day text-critic were those which concerned Origen. Origen was not attempting to reconstruct the original OG as would a modern text-critic who attempts to come as close as possible to the historically original translation; rather, he had a static view of the Hebrew and Greek texts and was seeking to arrive at what he believed to be the divinely inspired translation. In his view, the text of the Hebrew Bible had never undergone change, and, although he knew the Greek text could become corrupted, he believed that it began as a miraculously produced translation which agreed with the *hebraica veritas*. S. Brock reminds us that Origen was

> concerned with finding out what was the text of the Old Testament as used by Jews of *his own day* and since contact between Christians and Jews would naturally be near Greek speaking Jews, Origen's chief interest lay in the εκδοσεις of the Old Testament current in the Greek speaking Diaspora, that is to say, "The Three," Aquila, Theodotion, and Symmachus.[13]

Thus, Origen saw his task to be the restoration of the text circulating in his day as "the Septuagint" to its original state as the uncorrupted translation of the seventy elders which would then be identical with the Hebrew text which, he believed, existed at the time of the translation and continued unchanged unto his own day. This would enable Christians, in their debates with Jews, to use the OG translation authoritatively. The Jews' polemic, as the Christians saw it, was that the Christians falsified the Scriptures by using unacceptable translations, and Origen wanted to provide a Greek translation which would escape the imputation of error. Since Origen not only accepted the unchanging quality of the Hebrew uncritically, but also assumed that the Greek was corrupt when it diverged from the Semitic "original," he included insertions from θ' and α' in order to make the Greek conform to the Semitic text current in his day, thereby compounding errors in the true OG.

The θ' text is based on the OG but is a recension of it. Thus, θ' sometimes preserves the OG intact, wherever, through conscious choice, inadvertence, or inconsistency, the recensionist allowed the basic text to stand unrevised. At other times, θ' revises the OG according to systematic principles, in order to make it conform to the contemporary Semitic text of the day in a more standardized way.

Not cognizant of these variables, Origen sometimes changes the original text in light of readings in θ', α', or the Hebrew itself, and thus his fifth column, the intended "Septuagint" (= o', or "seventy") no longer preserves the OG. Conversely, there are also instances wherein θ' does indeed preserve

---

[13] S. Brock, "Origen's Aims as a Textual Critic of the Old Testament," *Studies in the Septuagint: Origins, Recensions, and Interpretations* (ed. S. Jellicoe; New York: Ktav, 1974) 344.

the OG (places where it did not change the OG for purposes of standardization), but since Origen has revised or erred, the LXX column no longer preserves it. Thus, in some instances the OG will be found in the θ′ text but not in the ο′ text. When Origen noted what he considered an addition in the OG he would mark the beginning of the reading with an obelus and the end of the reading with a metobelus. If he noted what he considered an omission in the Greek text, he would insert the missing text based upon the reading from other Greek texts or from the Hebrew/Aramaic text, marking the reading with an asterisk at the beginning and a metobelus at the end. However, in the course of transmitting the Hexapla, the sigla were not always recorded accurately, and other scribal errors occurred. In order to return to the OG, it is axiomatic to excise the alterations of Origen. Ziegler's masterful Göttingen edition attempts to arrive at the most accurate version of the OG by utilizing the LXX column of Origen as it is witnessed in 88–Syh, while comparing these readings with 967, patristic quotations, and θ′, α′, σ′, as well as by correcting obvious errors which have crept into the tradition by constant copying. Ziegler labels his OG text ο′ (= LXX). Besides utilizing Ziegler's text, we have examined the style of later recensionists (α′, σ′,θ′) in order to compare the less standardized style of the OG, and have also examined the OG vocabulary and style.[14] Ziegler's judgments concerning the OG readings as well as our disagreements with him are based upon accepted text-critical judgments, but there are occasions where the OG cannot be determined unequivocally.

88–Syh

Only one complete Greek manuscript is extant which witnesses to the ο′ text of Origen, namely, the complete Chisian manuscript, the Chigi, which is dated to the ninth-eleventh centuries c.e. This manuscript is numbered 88 in A. Rahlfs and Ziegler, and (erroneously) 87 in H. Swete.[15]

There is also extant the literal Syriac translation, the Syro-Hexapla (Syh), of the fifth column of Origen's Hexapla done by Paul of Tella in 615–617. Ziegler concludes that there is indeed a close relationship between these sister-manuscripts, which in fact preserve common mistakes. The Syriac will sometimes change word order, but this is in keeping with Syriac idiom and does not reflect true variants.

---

[14] Indispensable, though not perfect tools are J. Reider, *An Index to Aquila,* revised N. Turner (VTSup 12; Leiden: Brill, 1966) and E. Hatch and H. Redpath, *A Concordance to the Septuagint* (3 vols.; Oxford: Clarendon, 1897).

[15] A. Rahlfs, ed. *Septuaginta, Id est Vetus Testamentum graece iuxta LXX interpretes* (2 vols.; Stuttgart: Deutsche Bibelgesellschaft, 1982). H. B. Swete, *The Old Testament in Greek according to the Septuagint* (3 vols.; Cambridge: University, 1896).

In most places 88 and Syh preserve the same placement of obeli, asterisks, and metobeli.[16] Ziegler concludes that Syh is the more accurate when they differ in the placement of these symbols.

Papyrus 967

967 has been known since 1931 and is of great interest in reconstructing the OG of Daniel since it is the only pre-Hexaplaric Greek manuscript of Daniel available. The sections of 967 containing Daniel were brought to England, Cologne, and Barcelona, and have been published in four distinct works.[17] This manuscript has been dated by F. G. Kenyon to no later than the first half of the third century as the *terminus ad quem*. For the *terminus a quo* W. Hamm suggests 130 c.e. Although 967 often confirms that 88–Syh is accurate in its textual readings and its placement of asterisks and metobeli, it does provide interesting variants. As with any manuscript, these variants must be used judiciously. Some are original readings, but others are simply errors or glosses. Original readings in 967 include: 7:13 προσηγαγον] "they presented" παρησαν "they were present" 88–Syh^{txt}; 9:2 κυριου] "Lord" τη γη "the earth" 88–Syh; and 9:26 βασιλευς] "king" βασιλεια "kingdom." Errors in 967 include: 9:19 ιερουσαλημ "Jerusalem"] ισραηλ "Israel" 88–Syh and 11:4 της γης] "of the earth" του ουρανου "of heaven" 88–Syh.[18] In addition to the direct witnesses of 88–Syh and 967, indirect evidence is found in quotations of early Christian literature, some of which may be judged to come from the OG, or from a tradition close to it and distinct from θ′. These references are utilized throughout Ziegler's work and may be found in his extensive apparatus.

Witnesses to the θ′ Text of Daniel

Several uncial and minuscule manuscripts are extant which preserve θ′.[19] Rahlfs's edition is now superseded by Ziegler's Göttingen edition, which

---

[16] Ziegler (*Susanna, Daniel, Bel et Draco*, 13) reports that of 48 asterisks found, 37 are identical in 88 and in the Syro-Hexapla, and 11 belong to the Syro-Hexapla alone. Of 38 obeli, 34 are identical in both manuscripts, and 4 are found in the Syro-Hexapla alone.

[17] A. Geissen, *Der Septuaginta-Text des Buches Daniel nach dem Kölner Teil des Papyrus 967: Kap. V–XII* (Papyrologische Texte und Abhandlungen 5; Bonn: Habelt, 1968). W. Hamm, *Der Septuaginta-Text des Buches Daniel nach dem Kölner Teil des Papyrus 967: Kap. I–II* (Papyrologische Texte und Abhandlungen 10; Bonn: Habelt, 1969); *Kap. III–IV* (Papyrologische Texte und Abhandlungen 21; Bonn: 1977). R. Roca-Puig, "Daniele: Due semifogli del codice 967," *Aegyptus* 56 (1976) 3–18. See also F. Kenyon, *The Chester Beatty Biblical Papyri*, fasc. 1, 7 texts and pls. (London: Walker, 1938).

[18] The papyrus leaves apparently were separated without any particular order. For a listing of the contents of the papyrus, see Geissen, *Der Septuaginta-Text*, 12–16.

[19] For a complete listing see Ziegler, *Susanna, Daniel, Bel et Draco*, 28–31.

utilizes manuscripts critically and provides an eclectic text. θ′ is also quoted in several Greek Fathers, and these citations are also included in the critical apparatus of Ziegler.[20]

The History and Stratigraphy of the Text of Daniel

Theoretical Considerations

Identifying the history and stratigraphy of the book of Daniel is actually a subdivision of the theory of textual development of the Hebrew Bible and its translational and recensional history postulated since the discoveries of the Judaean wilderness, including Murabaat, Nahal Ḥever, and Qumran.[21]

Before 1947 only two sources were available for identifying what the Hebrew/Aramaic text of Daniel would have looked like before standardization processes and canonicity halted its growth and development. They are the Masoretic Text, a medieval text which has ancient roots in one pre-standardized tradition, and the ο′ text in so far as it preserves the OG which translates a pre-standardized *Vorlage*. Other witnesses: α′, σ′, θ′, the Vulgate, the Syriac, other daughter versions, and Patristic and Rabbinic citations come from a period of the beginning of the standardization period after the turn of the era.

With the discovery of the Qumran manuscripts a new set of sources demonstrates the fluidity of texts available to Jewish communities prior to standardization. Though the case may be different for parts or all of Daniel 1–6, we agree with E. Tov that it is not accurate to speak of textual types for Daniel 7–12. The evidence is not sufficient to warrant claims that Dan M, Q, G have characteristics which fall into patterns that can be identified as belonging to a particular locale or that these texts have typological differences which enable us to claim that Dan M follows a typological pattern seen

---

[20] Ibid. 32–35.

[21] Important studies include the following. D. Barthélemy, "L'ancien Testament a mûri à Alexandrie," and "Notes critiques sur quelques points d'histoire du texte," *Etudes d'histoire du Texte de l'Ancien Testament* (ed. D. Barthélemy, OBO 21; Göttingen: Vandenhoeck & Ruprecht, 1978) 127–40, 289–303. F. M. Cross, "The History of the Biblical Text in the Light of Discoveries in the Judaean Desert," *HTR* 57 (1964) 281–99; "The Evolution of a Theory of Local Texts," *Qumran and the History of the Biblical Text* (ed. F. M. Cross; Cambridge: Harvard University, 1975) 306–20. S. Talmon, "Aspects of the Textual Transmission of the Bible in the Light of Qumran Manuscripts," *Qumran and the History of the Biblical Text*, 226–63; and "The Textual Study of the Bible – A New Outlook," *Qumran and the History of the Biblical Text*, 321–400.

in M of other biblical books, or that Dan G must be linked with G of other books, or that Dan Q follows a particular "text type."[22] Rather, the relationship of M, Q, and θ' of Daniel to each other is complex; every text has both agreements and disagreements with the others.[23]

Although the oldest recoverable Semitic text of Daniel (H) can only be posited, the three available witnesses (M, Q, and G) yield readings which can be assumed most closely to approximate or preserve it. Although the question of an Urtext is debated we agree that the development of the Hebrew text began at some point soon after its written composition. We also note, however, that when judgments are made in individual readings concerning which witness is "original," the claim must rest on the presupposition that the author of the autograph composed (or edited together) only one version of the text. Text-critics are not wont to consider the possibility that an author or editor could have written more than one version of any individual work. We suggest that this should be considered. The existence of more than one version of a work occurs in other fields of artistic endeavor. George Frederick Handel and Thomas Cole, for example, composed and painted two versions of their works very close in time. Their second "copies" should not be considered revisions; rather, they simply fulfilled the demand for another exemplar. Since the ability to write was such a prized skill, it is conceivable that the authors of books of the Hebrew Bible themselves wrote more than one version. Thus, especially when variants do not preserve noteworthy alterations of meaning, two distinct readings could come from the same author, and both could be considered "original," or with equal claims as "preferable." In addition, if we think of the author as an editor or redactor of oral traditions, or of various written traditions, or a combination of these two, more than one version of the text, both with equal claim of being preferable, may indeed have come from the author's hands. Of course, it would be impossible to test this suggestion empirically with the biblical texts. In spite of this reservation about the judgment of original readings, we may proceed with text-critical judgments about individual readings if we accept the hypothesis that translations and recensions do indeed make changes as they develop over time. M, Q, and G must be examined on their own terms without a priori prejudice toward the so-called purity of M and the contention that the others are necessarily aberrant. One must keep in mind that M itself is one text among others.

---

[22] E. Tov, *The Text Critical Use of the Septuagint in Biblical Research* (Jerusalem Biblical Studies 3; Jerusalem: Simor, 1981) 272–75.

[23] Aware of these cautions and uncertainties we proceed to examine the relationships between these texts and judge individual readings.

The aspect of the theory which we find important is that an original Hebrew text underwent independent developments before standardization and that M, Q, and the *Vorlage* of G independently develop from H. This we accept and use as a working hypothesis for this study of Daniel. For Daniel, no Samaritan tradition is available; the witnesses to the Semitic text are M, 1QDan, 4QDan[a,b,c], and 6QDan, and the *Vorlage* of the OG in so far as it may be reconstructed.

Oral Stage

We may postulate that the textual history of Daniel may be traced back to its oral prehistory. References to Daniel in the book of Ezekiel (Ezek 14:14, 20; 28:3) are brief, but this information as well as the traditions of Dan'el from the Canaanite Aqhat myths show that the name and legends associated with it were familiar to persons in the land of Israel at least at a point much earlier than Daniel's written composition.[24] Moreover, the Prayer of Nabonidus and the OG of Daniel 4–6 appear to preserve an alternate form of the legend of Nebuchadnezzar found in M of Daniel 4, which may ultimately go back to oral tradition.

First Written Form

There is a consensus that the date for the completion of the Book of Daniel is between 168 and 163 B.C.E. The debate concerning its composition in Aramaic or Hebrew and subsequent translation into the alternate language continues. For this study we note that the witnesses to the original written text, M and Q, agree that the Aramaic begins in 2:4 and ends in 7:26. We now comment on the characteristics of the Semitic text of Daniel.

Subsequent Hebrew/Aramaic Textual Forms

The earliest forms of the text of Daniel from which preserved manuscripts are derived include M, Q, and the posited *Vorlage* of the OG.

In the past, M in general has been defined as short, non-conflate and non-expansionist. We hesitate to provide an over-all assessment of M of Daniel since this would involve an extensive examination of M and the subsequent translations and recensions of other books of the Hebrew Bible. Similarly, we do not propose to link the data from the Qumran fragments of Daniel to other scrolls of Qumran, nor do we attempt to identify the OG of Daniel as belonging to the same translational type found in another book. Rather, we offer some comparative statements or examples about M, Q, and

---

[24] See references to Daniel and Dan'el in 1 Chr 3:1, Ezra 8:2, and Neh 10:7 [6].

G of Daniel based solely on the way they appear in themselves or with a comparison of other transcriptions and translations of Daniel alone.

Commentators have pointed out previously that there are verses of Daniel in M which are corrupt and which defy any reconstruction that can be assured for its accuracy. Dan 8:11-12, 10:20b-21, and 11:1 are prime examples.[25] Moreover, our study of 4QDan shows that the superiority or inferiority of readings must be judged individually with reference to other versions and to the context. We offer the following examples. In 8:5 M correctly reads על פני "upon my face," where 4QDan^a has אל פני "toward my face"; in 11:15 M has the converted imperfect וישפך whereas 4QDan^{a,c} has the preferred converted perfect ושפך (from שפך, "pour out").

Some variants may be purely orthographic such as Dan 5:7 where M reads יקרה כתבה, 4QDan^a has יקר[א כתבא "reads [this] writing." Variants may offer no true change in the text such as 1:16 M את פתבגם ויין, 4QDan^a [את] פתבנ[ג]ם ואת [ויי]ן "their food and the wine." Variants may show additions or omissions in Q or omissions in M, such as in 5:7 where we find:

M	כשדיא		לאשפיא
4QDan^a	חרטמיא כ[ש]דיא		לאשפיא
ο′	τους επαοιδους και φαρμακους και χαλδαιους		
θ′	μαγους		χαλδαιους

Note that θ′ follows the *Vorlage* of M "the enchanters, the Chaldeans" whereas ο′ = Q "the enchanters, the magicians, and the Chaldeans." Or, variants may show that different readings existed in M and Q, such as in Dan 8:1 where M reads חזון נראה "a vision appeared," and 4QDan^a reads ד[ב]ר נגלה חזון נראה. The crossed out words, ד[ב]ר נגלה "a matter was revealed" may point to a text which had this reading only and not חזון נראה. The OG *Vorlage* of Daniel 7-12 appears to be roughly the same as M and Q. When variants are extant in Q, and when ο′ differs from H, we examine the possibility that an alternative *Vorlage* might most adequately account for the variant. This is the case in general for chapters 4-6 of Daniel and in individual readings elsewhere.

Hebrew Scribal Copying

In some instances, a superior reading is found in Q or G because M contains an error made from scribal additions or omissions to the Hebrew tradition. For example, in Dan 7:11 we find

---

[25] J. Montgomery, *A Critical and Exegetical Commentary on the Book of Daniel* (ICC; Edinburgh: T. & T. Clark, 1927) 335, 356-58. Hartman and Di Lella, *The Book of Daniel*, 265-66, 285-86.

M חזה הוית עד די קטילת חיותא
o′, 967 και απετυμπανισθη το θηριον
θ′ εως ανηρεθη το θηριον

The possible implications of the meaning of the OG translation are discussed in Chapter V. We note at this point, however, that both o′ and θ′ witness to the fact that חזה הוית "I beheld" was not in their respective *Vorlagen*. We should consider the M reading to be a scribal addition to H, stemming from the previous חזה הוית in the beginning of 7:11.

In 8:14 the texts read:

M ויאמר אלי
o′, 967 και ειπεν αυτω
θ′ και ειπεν αυτω

We suggest that אלו "to him" was the original reading, showing an early orthography; o′ and θ′ reflect אלו or its later, *plene* form אליו. M errs, as the context shows, with אלי "to me," presumably due to simple scribal confusion of *waw* and *yod*.[26] These examples caution us to consider the possibility that the most preferred reading could be found in a witness other than M, and that the M reading varies from the original H due to understandable scribal alterations.

Having sketched the development of the text of Daniel from its oral stage to its first written form, to its subsequent Semitic textual forms, and its additional Hebrew changes in scribal copying, we are now able to offer some statements about its translation and recension into Greek.

The Date and Character of the OG

Dating the OG of Daniel is hampered by the paucity of evidence and by the additional problem that what does exist is unreliable. It has been customary to date the OG of Daniel to a period shortly after its autograph (168–163 B.C.E.) since 1 Maccabees putatively contains verses which reflect the OG. This argument was first suggested by Bludau and repeated with modifications by both J. Montgomery and Di Lella.[27] Di Lella agrees with Montgomery and Bludau that four "phrases of LXX-Daniel appear in the Greek text of 1 Maccabees" and concludes:

---

[26] Cf. אלו in 4QSamᶜ. See E. Ulrich, "4QSamᶜ: A Fragmentary Manuscript of 2 Samuel 14–15 from the Scribe of the *Serek Hay-yaḥad* (1QS)," *BASOR* 235 (1979) 1–25, esp. pp. 3,5,7.

[27] A. Bludau, "Die alexandrinische Uebersetzung des Buches Daniel," 8. Di Lella, *The Book of Daniel*, 78.

from this evidence it can rightly be assumed that LXX-Dn goes back to at least the date of the Greek texts of 1 Maccabees. As 1 Maccabees, originally composed in Hebrew, was translated into Greek no earlier than 100 B.C., we may safely conclude that LXX-Daniel originated at about that time.[28]

We now examine these cited passages:

(1)

1 Macc 1:9		επληθυναν κακα εν τη γη
Dan 12:4	o′	πλησθη η γη αδικιας
	θ′	πληθυνθη η γνωσις

(2)

1 Macc 1:18		και επεσον τραυματιαι πολλοι
Dan 11:26	o′	και πεσουνται τραυματιαι πολλοι
	θ′	και πεσουνται τραυματιαι πολλοι

(3)

1 Macc 4:41		καθαριση τα αγια
1 Macc 4:43		εκαθαρισαν τα αγια
Dan 8:14	o′	καθαρισθησεται το αγιον
	θ′	καθαρισθησεται το αγιον

(4)

1 Macc 1:54		βδελυγμα ερημωσεως
Dan 11:31	o′	βδελυγμα ερημωσεως
	θ′	βδελυγμα ερημωσεως

The first three phrases do not point to true literary dependence of 1 Maccabees upon the OG of Daniel. In the first example, although the verbs come from the same root, they are in different forms; η γη is the subject of the phrase in Dan 12:4 whereas it is the object of the preposition εν in 1 Macc 1:9, and the word choice to represent the concept "evil" are totally distinct. If 1 Maccabees were quoting Dan 12:4 one would not expect these alterations. In the second example, again the verbal tenses are distinct, and in the third example, not only are the verbal tenses different, but αγιος is found in different forms.

Even more important than the grammatical changes is the recognition that such phrases as "evils were multiplied on the earth," and "many were wounded unto death" were common expressions from the period of Antiochus's persecution; moreover, they are found in other biblical texts outside of Daniel. To assert that they signify direct borrowing is clearly an

---

[28] Di Lella, *The Book of Daniel*, 78.

exaggeration.[29] Only the fourth example, βδελυγμα ερημωσεως "abomination of desolation" is found both in 1 Maccabees and in Daniel; nevertheless, a two word phrase does not signify direct borrowing. The phrase appears to be a slogan or rallying cry by which the community underscored their plight. When θ′ revised ο′ the expression was retained in all three occurrences (Dan 9:27, 11:31, 12:11) which may point to its continuing popular usage. Similarly, Mark 13:14 uses the two word phrase without placing it in the Daniel context. Montgomery states that the phrase "may have arisen contemporaneously with Antiochus' sacrilege"[30] and it may well have been the typical way by which pious Jews referred to the altar or statue which Antiochus had set up in the Temple. To base an argument for 1 Maccabees's literary dependency on the OG of Daniel by one phrase would go beyond the evidence.

Rather than searching for evidence in putative quotations to date the OG of Daniel we must examine the period of time wherein translational activity was taking place. The *Letter of Aristeas,* Ben Sira, and the colophon of Greek Esther show that translations of the Hebrew text into Greek were made starting in the third-second centuries B.C.E. and continued thereafter. Although these texts do not give evidence that translations were made in these centuries alone, they do provide a context in which it is possible to posit the translation of Daniel into Greek at some time shortly after its autograph. Even more important for a relative dating of the OG of Daniel are the latter recensional developments of α′, σ′, and θ′ which may be used to set the outermost limits of the translation, since they would postdate the OG.

Although the *Letter of Aristeas* is laced with legendary material, it does indicate that the translation of the Pentateuch was being undertaken by at least the third or second century B.C.E. E. Bickerman suggests a date for the latter between 145–127 B.C.E. because of greeting formulae, names of court officers, and other formal characteristics which correspond to papyri of the second century B.C.E.[31] The actual composition of the *Letter of Aristeas* itself indicates that by the second century, and possibly earlier, "Alexandrian Jewry attained a sufficient degree of Hellenization to create Jewish literature in Greek [and] there were Jewish writers in Alexandria who wrote on Jewish subjects for the Jewish reader in Greek."[32] If Jews were composing in Greek

---

[29] For the first set of phrases above we note the following similar references in the Bible: Gen 6:11 and 6:13 have επλησθη η γη αδικιας and Jer 28 (51):5 has η γη αυτων επλησθη αδικιας. For the second set of readings noted above we find the phrases επεσον τραυματιαι πολλοι in Judg 9:40, ηρξατο πατασσειν τραυματιας in Judg 20:39, and τραυματιαι πολλοι επεσον in 1 Chr 5:22.

[30] J. Montgomery, *A Critical and Exegetical Commentary,* 38.

[31] E. Bickerman, "Zur Datierung des Pseudo-Aristeas," *ZNW* 29 (1930) 280–98.

[32] V. Tcherikover, "The Ideology of the Letter of Aristeas," *Studies in the Septuagint,* 182.

it is not surprising that the Scriptures were being translated as well. If the Pentateuch was being translated during the third-second centuries B.C.E., it would be likely that additional Jewish books were translated shortly thereafter.

The colophon to the Greek version of Esther provides another reference point for dating the translations of Hebrew books into Greek. The colophonist states that a Greek translation of Esther was completed "by Lysimachus son of Ptolemy, a member of the Jerusalem community." C. Moore suggests that the opening phrase of the colophon, "In the fourth year of the reign of Ptolemy and Cleopatra" refers to Ptolemy VIII, Soter II (ca. 114 B.C.E.), although the reference could refer to other Ptolemies, such as Ptolemy XII and Ptolemy XIV (ca. 77 B.C.E. and 48 B.C.E.). While doubts remain as to which Ptolemy is meant and to which Greek version of Esther the colophon applies, the colophon itself is authentic and provides another example of second-first century B.C.E. translation.[33]

R. Klein refers to three ancient authors who also attest to the existence of an OG translation of the Hebrew Scriptures.[34] Demetrius, who wrote at the end of the third century B.C.E., quotes Genesis according to the translation of the Septuagint. Eupolemes of the second century B.C.E. refers to the Septuagint of Chronicles, and 1 Maccabees preserves the Psalms of the Old Greek.

The Prologue to Ben Sira (ca. 130 B.C.E.) indicates that not only was this work itself translated into Greek but apparently the translator was familiar with translations of other biblical books since the text reads, "The Law itself, and the Prophets, and the rest of the books have no small difference when they are spoken in their original form" (Prologue). These texts show that the translation of the Semitic text of Daniel into Greek is possible and plausible at a point shortly after its written composition, although we cannot state with certainty how soon after the composition it was completed.

Perhaps the best way to date the translation is by a relative chronology. Our understanding of Greek recensional history also sheds light on the date of the OG which must antedate α', σ', and θ'. We accept the hypothesis of one major OG translation which later formed the basis for revisions and recensions, that is, systematic revisions according to established principles in order to bring the Greek into closer conformity with the Hebrew text of the recensionists' time. A crucial study which forms the basis of this theory is the work of D. Barthélemy on the Greek Scroll of the Minor Prophets (called

---

[33] C. Moore, *Daniel, Esther, and Jeremiah: the Additions* (AB 44; Garden City: Doubleday, 1977) 250. Cf. *Esther* (AB 7B; Garden City: Doubleday, 1971) 112–13.

[34] R. Klein, *Textual Criticism of the Old Testament* (Guides to Biblical Scholarship; Philadelphia: Fortress, 1974) 2–3.

"R") discovered in 1952 in Nahal Ḥever, in which he demonstrated that recensional activity was undertaken to align the OG with M (or its proto-type).[35] This scroll has been paleographically dated to the second half of the first century B.C.E. based upon Greek scripts and paleo-Hebrew inserts. If recensions were being made by this time, the translations into Greek must have been made earlier. Again, it is possible and plausible that the transla-tion of Daniel into Greek predates this period.

This recension, named either "R" or χαιγε (because of the use of this word for the Hebrew גם) postdates the OG and antedates the text of α′ (early second century C.E.). It is not limited to R, however, but is found in sections of both the fifth and sixth columns of the Hexapla. For example, it is found in the fifth ("LXX") column of parts of Samuel–Kings, where it was substituted for the original OG in 2 Sam 11:2–1 Kgs 2:11 and 1 Kgs 22–2 Kgs. For sixth column exemplars, Barthélemy suggests Lamentations, Canticles, Ruth, the Vaticanus family of Judges, the Theodotion text of Daniel and the additions to Job, the anonymous additions to Jeremiah, and the Quinta of Psalms.

Barthélemy's theory has since been tested by such studies as those of K. O'Connell and W. Bodine who unravelled the development of the Greek texts of Exodus and Judges respectively, and delineate their recensional activity.

O'Connell's *The Theodotionic Revision of the Book of Exodus* investi-gates the sixth column in Exodus and concludes that it too is "related to Barthélemy's χαιγε recension and is to be regarded as an integral part of that recension."[36] Moreover, he shows that these readings "come from a careful and generally consistent revision of an already partially revised form of the OG to a Hebrew text virtually identical with the present MT," which was used later by Aquila as the basis of one further recension.[37]

Bodine tests Barthélemy's position that the Vaticanus (B) family of the Greek texts of Judges also belongs to the χαιγε recension. Besides testing Barthélemy's criteria for identifying the χαιγε recension in Judges, Bodine identifies additional distinguishing characteristics of the B family of Judges, both "those which appear elsewhere in the χαιγε recension and then those which are peculiar to the B family of Judges.[38] Bodine concludes that "the

[35] D. Barthélemy, "Récouverte d'un chaînon manquant de l'histoire de la Septante," *RB* 60 (1953) 18–29.

[36] K. O'Connell, *The Theodotionic Revision of the Book of Exodus* (HSM 3; Cambridge: Harvard University, 1972) 5.

[37] Ibid.

[38] W. R. Bodine, *The Greek Text of Judges* (HSM 23, Chico: Scholars, 1980) 5.

Judges sixth column has a form of the Old Greek as its base"[39] and that "the base text has undergone extensive revision toward MT."[40] He also concludes that the sixth column readings of Judges "has been extensively revised to MT or to a Hebrew so close to MT that it cannot be distinguished."[41] Moreover, it "is not part of the καιγε recension,"[42] but comes from another reviser (perhaps the historical Theodotion) who, using the OG, "perceived the need for revision to be extensive."[43]

Thus, in comparing ο' and θ' of Daniel when making judgments about the true OG and θ' dependence on the OG, the characteristics and vocabulary identified by Barthélemy, O'Connell, and Bodine may be used for testing criteria (as in Chapter II), and for identifying recensional changes from the OG in the ο' and θ' texts. For Daniel 7-12, this study confirms the hypothesis that θ', the earliest complete witness to recensional activity in Daniel, is not a separate translation of the Hebrew, but is rather a recension, since so many of the θ' readings are equivalent to ο' and thus shows dependency upon the OG, whereas the differences are predominantly consistent systematization of revisions toward M. We present detailed examples in Chapter II.

The Date and Character of θ'

The dating of the θ' text is debatable. The historical Theodotion has been dated to the second century c.e. since Irenaeus (d. ca. 202) identifies him as an Ephesian who completed a Greek translation, and Epiphanius (d. 392) records that he lived during Commodus's reign (approximately 180 c.e.). Yet the information of Epiphanius is contradicted by Irenaeus who implies that Theodotion completed his translation before Aquila (ca. 130 c.e.).[44] Moreover, the dating of the θ' text is problematic both because it is quoted in the New Testament, which precedes the date of the historical Theodotion, and because of the evidence that the θ' text of Daniel belongs to the καιγε recension, which precedes the recensional activity of Aquila.[45] Of the θ' text, Cross notes that "Daniel, traditionally assigned to Theodotion, and correctly recognized by a number of scholars as 'Proto-Theodotion'. . . was an early Jewish attempt to revise the standard LXX into conformity with

[39] Ibid., 141.
[40] Ibid., 143.
[41] Ibid., 148.
[42] Ibid., 147.
[43] Ibid., 149.
[44] Montgomery, *A Critical and Exegetical Commentary*, 46-47.
[45] Cross, "History of the Biblical Text," 178. See also Barthélemy, *Les devanciers d'Aquila* (VTSup 10; Leiden: Brill, 1963) and O'Connell, *The Theodotionic Revision of the Book of Exodus*.

Review of Literature

Bludau's examination of 1897 remained the fullest study on the OG of Daniel until McCrystall's dissertation of 1980.[53] Bludau's study presupposes that the *Vorlage* of the OG was M, that the OG is equivalent to the o′ text, and that o′ and θ′ represent two distinct translations of the Hebrew. Because of these methodological presuppositions, Bludau proceeds to compare the text with M, and when he notes differences, he consistently concludes that they are to be accounted for by the theological motivation of the translator. He does not explore the possibility that they were prompted by a Semitic *Vorlage* of the OG at times distinct from M, that they reflect misreadings of the OG, or that the o′ text preserves simply inadvertent later developments of the OG. Even when a metathesis is noted, for example, Bludau concludes that the OG intentionally changed the letters for a distinct theological claim.

We turn now to one of Bludau's more salient examples which is representative of his method:

9:24

M   ולמשח קדש קדשים
o′   και ευφραναι αγιον αγιων
θ′   και του χρισαι αγιον αγιων

Concerning the variant in o′, Bludau argues that this text does not reflect the events of the time period of the author of the Hebrew text, but rather the later date of the OG translator who lived during Judas Maccabeus's triumph. Even though Bludau acknowledges that ευφραναι "to exult" can be accounted for with a metathesis, ולמשח "to anoint" > ולשמח "to exult," he argues that the verb ευφραναι, which refers to the rejoicing over the fulfillment of Jeremiah's prophecy, makes sense only if it refers to a person, and not to a thing or place (as it does in M).[54] He concludes that the phrase αγιον αγιων "holy of holies" refers to Daniel himself or to the high priest who is to lead the Jews out of imprisonment. However, we would assess this variant as coming from the simple mechanical error. לשמח either was present in a *Vorlage* which had already made the error, or came from the OG translator who confused the letters. If the variant is intentional on the part of the translator it may reveal what he thought to be theologically possible; however, the context makes clear that the OG translator retained the sense of the remainder of the verse and was not otherwise engaging in intentional

---

[53] Bludau, "Die alexandrinische Uebersetzung des Buches Daniel," and A. McCrystall, "Studies in the Old Greek Translation of Daniel," unpublished doctoral dissertation (University of Oxford: 1980).

[54] Bludau, "Die alexandrinische Uebersetzung des Buches Daniel," 107.

theological *Tendenz*. The following verse (9:25) shows that it is indeed the Temple to which the author and translator are referring, for here we read of the rebuilding of Jerusalem. Moreover 9:26 states και βασιλεια εθνων φθερει την πολιν και το αγιον "and the kingdom of the nations will destroy the city and the sanctuary." Though ευφραναι could be interpreted in isolation as either stemming from metathesis or as being theologically motivated, the continuing translation of this chapter of Daniel clearly indicates the former and belies the latter.

Overall, Bludau concludes that the translation of the OG of Daniel, with the exception of Daniel 4–6 was free, yet accurate, though laced with examples of theological *Tendenz*. He concludes that for Daniel 4–6 the frequent discrepancies are due to the translator's own perspective and does not argue that he worked from a distinct *Vorlage*. For the rest of Daniel, the most important example of theological *Tendenz* is to be found in 9:24–27. We examine his arguments below in Chapter V.

Montgomery's commentary of 1927 continues to be an excellent contribution for the study of manuscripts available at his time, the history of the texts, and for the insightful literary, historical, and textual investigation of Daniel.[55] Although Montgomery does not set out to provide an investigation of the OG as a whole, his textual notes often provide brilliant assessment of the genesis of variants. Montgomery's individual judgments can be improved upon, however, because of new manuscript evidence and because of our knowledge of textual stratigraphy. For example, in his assessment of the textual variant in 8:4 Montgomery suggests that the OG translator had additional information concerning the kingdoms of the east which might account for the exegetical plus of προς ανατολας "to the east" when listing the directions toward which the ram, symbolizing Persia, charges.[56] An extended discussion of the variant is found in Chapter V. For now we note that our reconstruction of the *Vorlage* from which the OG is translated is enhanced by 4QDan[a] which includes מזרחה "to the east," and 967 which preserves the listing of the directions in a different order than that found in o'. Montgomery entertains the possibility of a distinct *Vorlage* only in assessing chapters 4–6. But in general, Montgomery concludes with Bludau that the OG is a fairly accurate translation, although he notes "the presence of genuine glosses, both primary and secondary, which may occur lines away from their proper destination . . . and also of doublet translations."[57] Thus, in principle, Montgomery distinguishes between the OG and the developed o', although he does not always specify this process as such nor investigate

[55] Montgomery, *A Critical and Exegetical Commentary*.
[56] Ibid., 328.
[57] Ibid., 36.

the possibility often. He includes two detailed charts on the variants of 9:24-27 and 8:11-12 in which he does attempt to distinguish between the OG (which he calls "original G") and subsequent glosses or revisions.[58]

In debate with Montgomery is R. H. Charles's *Commentary on Daniel*.[59] Charles holds that the OG translation comes from an "earlier form of the Semitic text, of which the LXX form in the Chigi ms. presents us with a valuable, though corrupt rendering."[60] He believes that this is the case, not only for chapters 1-3 and 7-12, but also for 4-6. In several instances where o' singularly among the versions contains a phrase, Charles holds that this is valuable evidence for the original.[61] Charles rightly examines verses on an individual basis before he judges which is original and offers many helpful explanations. However, a methodological survey of his book shows several errors. He presumes that the OG follows the word order of its Semitic *Vorlage*. Thus, if the OG and M differ on this matter, he presumes that the OG is superior and judges M to be a later corruption, not taking into account the OG freedom with syntax. Also, in making his judgments concerning the reliability of a phrase in the OG versus its counterpart in M, he searches such phrases in other biblical and extra-biblical writings for the most frequent rendering without adequately taking into account the history of the tradition of the phrase or the possibility of redaction. For example, in his discussion of Dan 7:13, he claims that the o' reading επι των νεφελων "upon the clouds" and not the reading of θ' μετα των νεφελων = M "with the clouds" must be original because "the 'one like a son of man' comes not 'with' but 'on the clouds.' The clouds are not his companions (μετα) but the chariot as it were on which he approaches the Ancient of Days."[62] It is curious to note that Montgomery in selecting the basis for judgment about which preposition is original when talking about the Son of Man also wants to make the correct reading of 7:13 correspond to *theological* views of the clouds accompanying God. We would caution that knowing the use of a phrase is certainly helpful in formulating an opinion about which is preferable in Daniel. However, the judgment cannot simply be made on this basis, especially when the phrase in question is formulated in different ways throughout its history of usage. Similarly, Charles will often take a phrase in the OG as preferable, if he believes it is something consistent with what the author should know. This reading into the mind of the author sometimes seems to be characteristic

---

[58] Ibid., 356-58; 401-402.

[59] R. H. Charles, *A Critical and Exegetical Commentary on the Book of Daniel* (Oxford: Clarendon, 1929).

[60] Ibid., lvi.

[61] Ibid., lxi-lxviii.

[62] Ibid., 186.

of Charles's commentaries.[63] For example, in 7:17 the phrase "which are four" is present in M but omitted in the OG. Charles argues that the OG preserves an original reading since "the seer knows perfectly well the number of the kingdoms."[64] This type of argument goes beyond the evidence of the context and does not take into account the tendency of the OG translator to paraphrase some readings.

One of the more recent commentaries on the book of Daniel, Hartman and Di Lella's commentary, *The Book of Daniel,* basically confirms earlier studies in its method in dating the OG and in its notes on the differences in the o' text.[65] As in Montgomery's commentary, there is neither a comprehensive presentation nor any attempt to delineate the characteristics of the OG as a whole. The discussion of individual OG readings occurs singularly in the notes which are important for our discussion of significant variants and putative theological *Tendenz.* We now turn to a representative example.

7:13

M   עם עֲנֵי שְׁמַיָּא

   o'   επι των νεφελων του ουρανου

   θ'   μετα των νεφελων του ουρανου

Hartman believes that important distinct theological claims are made by the expressions עם עֲנֵי שְׁמַיָּא "with the clouds" = μετα των νεφελων του ουρανου, θ' and the OG επι των νεφελων του ουρανου "upon the clouds." An extended discussion is found below in Chapter V. For now we note that the assessment of the variant is made only by comparing the o' text with M in this single verse. The important factor of translation technique is lacking. Consideration of the OG translator's use of prepositions throughout Daniel 7-12, of textual variants for עם and על in other places of the Hebrew Bible, and of the history of the phrase "riding on the clouds" is necessary before assessing the probability of theological *Tendenz* on the part of the OG translator when this verse was translated.

For investigation of Daniel 7-12, P. Grélot's study, "Les versions greques de Daniel," is most informative.[66] Grélot notes that quotations of Daniel found in the New Testament and in other early Christian writings such as those of Justin and the Shepherd of Hermas sometimes reflect the o' text and at other times reflect θ'. Rather than arguing for a mixed Greek text or for a proto-θ' text Grélot believes that these Christian authors know

---

[63] See, for example, R. H. Charles, *The Assumption of Moses* (London: Adam and Charles Black, 1897).

[64] Charles, *A Critical and Exegetical Commentary,* 189.

[65] Hartman and Di Lella, *The Book of Daniel.*

[66] P. Grélot, "Les versions grecques de Daniel," *Biblica* 47 (1966) 381-402.

both of the distinct texts. θ′ has a stronger influence, yet the OG is still known.[67] Grélot holds that θ′ should be considered a recension and not a new translation and that it antedates α′.[68] However, since the Aramaic *Vorlage* of chapters 4–6 of θ′ is divergent from the *Vorlage* of ο′ for these chapters, Grélot concludes that θ′ might better be considered a "nouvelle version."[69] We agree that the *Vorlage* of 4–6 is indeed distinct and that consequently for sections of these chapters θ′ is translating some new passages. However, Grélot continues, "Pour les autres chapitres les divergences sont moindres; mais néanmoins il y a de telles différence dans le vocabulaire et les tournures comme dans la texture de certains versets qu'on peut parler d'une traduction entièrement refaite."[70] By calling Daniel θ′ "une traduction entièrement refaite" Grélot obscures the fact that a recensionist, such as θ′, if the occasion warrants, may indeed have to newly translate a word or phrase, but this is done by first comparing the OG to the Semitic *Vorlage* of the recensionist's day. To call Dan θ′ a new translation might veil the fact that the recensionist proceeds by this comparative effort and offers another translation only when it is deemed necessary according to the recensionist's principles of Greek equivalents of diction and syntax vis-à-vis his *Vorlage*.

We are in agreement with Grélot's argument both that the differences in the two Greek texts may indeed be prompted by variants in the *Vorlage* which may antedate the fixed Masoretic Text,[71] and that "Cette antiquité ne les rend pas nécessairement préférables à la recension massorétique: il faut en juger dans chaque cas particulier."[72]

More recent articles on the Old Greek translation of Daniel come from F. F. Bruce.[73] By comparing the meaning of the Greek text of ο′ with the Semitic text of Daniel, Bruce argues that the "Septuagint" of Daniel is a distinct paraphrastic interpretation of the Semitic text which preserves the earliest indication of the exegesis of the Book of Daniel. This Greek text of Daniel is part of several Greek translations of the Hebrew Scriptures, which "confirms the view that variants are not to be explained solely by the ordinary causes of textual alteration but sometimes reflect new ways of understanding the prophecies in the light of changing events, changing attitudes and

---

[67] Ibid., 390.
[68] Ibid., 392.
[69] Ibid., 394.
[70] Ibid., 395.
[71] Ibid., 399.
[72] Ibid.
[73] F. F. Bruce, "The Earliest Old Testament Interpretation," *OTS* 17 (1972) 37–52; "The Oldest Greek Version of Daniel," *OTS* 20 (1975) 22–40; "Prophetic Interpretation in the Septuagint," *BIOSCS* 12 (1979) 17–26.

changing exegetical methods."[74] In his reading of the o' text of Daniel 7–12, Bruce finds that the meaning of the Greek translation is distinctly interpretative in several passages. We cite the following salient examples of his conclusions. (1) Since the OG translator lived through the historical situation wherein the Romans demanded that Antiochus leave Egypt, the translator makes concrete reference to it in Dan 11:30.[75] (2) The OG translator "achieves some success in his attempt to be a helpful interpreter" in Dan 11:42 by identifying "the king of the south" as "the king of Egypt."[76] (3) The seventy years of Jerusalem's desolation is reinterpreted to seventy heptads of years to correspond more accurately with the translator's historical experience.[77] (4) An "astonishing alteration" of the original text is found in Dan 9:24–27 concerning the interpretation of the total time of Antionchus' oppression. A new total of 139 years replaces the Hebrew text's "sixty-two weeks."[78] (5) In the OG of Dan 9:6 "a note of wider universalism is struck" since "the prophets who spoke 'to all the people of the land' . . . are now said to have spoke 'to every nation on earth.'"[79] (6) The OG of Dan 7:13 preserves "an astonishing statement about the 'one like a son of man'—that he appeared 'as (the) Ancient of Days.'"[80] (7) The OG gives a new interpretation to the time of the end, as is evidenced in Dan 12:2, as Bruce remarks: "in the resurrection passage in Dan. xii 2 those who rise from their sleep . . . are divided into three, not two groups."[81] These observations lead Bruce to conclude that "the Theodotionic version is a straightforward translation whereas the Septuagint is a targumic-style paraphrase."[82]

By correctly noting the differences of meaning in the o' text of Daniel or in witnesses to the OG when compared to the Masoretic text, Bruce surely begins on the right path for investigating the possibility of theological *Tendenz* in the OG of Daniel. If his analysis of the OG is correct, one would have important clues for identifying the theological interests of a member of the diaspora as well as references to his historical situation and perhaps provide us with further evidence for understanding the way in which translators commented upon their sacred texts. However, before Bruce's arresting conclusions can be verified, they must survive further investigative tests. As the above delineation of the Greek texts has shown, one cannot always assume

[74] Bruce, "Prophetic Interpretation in the Septuagint," 26.
[75] Bruce, "The Earliest Old Testament Interpretation," 41–42.
[76] Ibid., 42–43.
[77] Ibid., 43.
[78] Ibid., 43–44.
[79] Ibid., 44.
[80] Bruce, "The Oldest Greek Version of Daniel," 24.
[81] Ibid., 25–26.
[82] Ibid., 38.

that the o′ text of Origen is equal to the OG, although in the majority of cases that is true. One must investigate the possibility of secondary additions, inner-Greek errors, as well as the characteristics of the OG of Daniel and the way in which it typically translates its Semitic *Vorlage* as a whole. Moreover, our understanding of the history of the Semitic text will assist in determining whether the Greek actually may be faithfully translating a distinct *Vorlage* which is no longer extant. Finally, a thorough investigation of other passages in Daniel which refer to the same or to similar themes or expressions needs to be undertaken.

Building on the suggestions of Bruce, McCrystall continues to investigate the differences in meaning of the text of o′ and M. His dissertation,[83] completed in 1980, includes an excellent, thorough review of the literature on the scholarly inquiry into the OG of Daniel, a brief investigation of the translation techniques of the OG, a unique comparison of the Greek vocabulary of the translator with that of contemporary papyri, a study of "a possible overall coherent chronological system which might have been used in Daniel MT or in Daniel OG,"[84] and a delineation of the so-called historicizing elements of the OG.

McCrystall's study of the translation technique of the OG finds that the OG of Daniel (1) does not use transliterations, as opposed to θ′, (2) chooses words to echo other passages of the Bible (such as πυλη and ωλαμ in Dan 8:2 to recall Ezekiel),[85] (3) is less literal in its translation than θ′, (4) "is so deviant as to necessitate a high level of independence from any tendency to uniformity dictated by the desire to keep close to the spirit of the Hebrew as seen in Daniel MT,"[86] and (5) contains variant readings which are indicative of the interpretative activity of the translator. His overall conclusion is that the OG translation has "the peculiarities of which some can only be accounted for by the activity of someone who was translating from a deliberate standpoint."[87]

Given the length of McCrystall's dissertation, it is not feasible to critique every example he has included for his study. However, the more important examples from Daniel 7–12 used as representative examples of the OG's distinct theological, historical, or political viewpoint will be discussed in the chapters which follow. Our method of investigation here is similar to the procedure for examining Bruce's claims. Like Bruce, McCrystall compares the meaning of the OG with that of the Hebrew. He does not fail to consider

---

[83] McCrystall, "Studies in the Old Greek Translation of Daniel."
[84] Ibid., iii.
[85] Ibid., 76.
[86] Ibid.
[87] Ibid.

what might have been the Hebrew *Vorlage,* but he does consistently conclude that the OG does not have a distinct *Vorlage* but rather reflects M. Our study of the Qumran texts of Daniel coupled with our knowledge of the stratigraphy of the texts provides more data to be investigated before we conclude that the OG is engaging in theological *Tendenz.* Moreover, we view the relationship between o′ and θ′ to be more complex than does McCrystall, and we provide a sample of their typical relationship in Chapter II, before we proceed with conclusions about possible theological *Tendenz.* We also note at this point that McCrystall does acknowledge that many of the readings in the OG which differ from the sense of M so occur because of metathesis, omitted or added letters, confusion of letters, and other such phenomena, which we would consider to be mechanical errors. However, McCrystall believes that mechanical changes are deliberately introduced in order that the translator may deal freely with the text and translate from a particular standpoint. Our position is that in order for this conception to be likely, we must investigate representatives of all mechanical changes, and not only those wherein distinct changes in theological, political, or historical meaning occur. In other words, we wish to investigate whether these metatheses and other text-critical phenomena might not truly be errors. Another control on this investigation is to examine the significant changes in their context. Is the same example of *Tendenz* found when the OG translator comes upon like ideas in other passages? If the change is deliberate, it is most reasonable to expect that it would be found in those instances where the same idea occurs.

II

THE CHARACTER AND ACCURACY
OF THE OLD GREEK

Having traced the history of the text of Daniel as well as some prevailing approaches to the study of the OG, we now turn to a study of the OG of Daniel itself. Our presupposition is that before claims about the theological *Tendenz* of the OG can be made, we must first have as full knowledge as possible of the character and accuracy of the OG in general. In order to come to this fuller understanding of the character of the OG, we have chosen two methods of investigation in this chapter. First, we have selected a sample continuous passage (Dan 8:1-10) to show in a word-by-word analysis the characteristics of the OG and θ′ as a point of reference for the OG. Secondly, so that our study is not limited to Dan 8:1-10 alone, we have selected test cases which are representative of the translation technique of the OG as a whole. While these examples are not exhaustive, they do provide an adequate foundation for assessing the general character and accuracy of the OG.

Sample Continuous Passage: Dan 8:1-10

Introduction

The first Hebrew section of Daniel 7-12 was selected for several reasons. First of all, most of Daniel 7-12 is written in Hebrew; thus a Hebrew passage is appropriate. Secondly, in general a Hebrew passage will yield more data than an Aramaic passage when making comparisons with Greek recensions, since it is easier to trace the standardization of a Hebrew root into Greek simply because there is far more Hebrew literature than Aramaic literature in the Bible. Thirdly, the passage is not laden with many OG readings interpreted by critics as based on theological *Tendenz* and thus should yield a typical picture of the OG; this is in contrast to the theological content of Daniel 7, 9, and 12, and the veiled historical content of chapter 11. Fourthly, the passage also is attested in several extant Hebrew fragments from 4QDan[a] and 4QDan[b], some of which are overlapping.

By investigating the way in which θ′ revises the OG we will see exactly where the two texts differ, shedding light on whether the revisions were made because of content or in accordance with well-known formal characteristics of the θ′ recension. We wish to uncover whether θ′ revises the OG in the interest of correcting what was perceived even back then as theological *Tendenz* in the OG or whether the revision is done, more neutrally, in the interest of lexical and grammatical fidelity.

In order to see the way in which θ′ either preserves or changes the OG which was used as the basis we now turn to our close reading of Dan 8:1-10. In the following pages of charts we have arranged the readings into the following way: columns with the Hebrew texts of M, 4QDan[a] and 4QDan[b] (in so far as the latter two are extant) are aligned with columns of the corresponding Greek texts of o′, 967, and θ′. In addition, we add an interpretive column labeled "commentary on θ′," in which a coded commentary on the θ′ revision of the OG is presented. Our code for the commentary is as follows: a = word order, where θ′ conforms the OG to the word order found in its Hebrew *Vorlage;* b = syntax, where θ′ alters the grammatical forms and style of the OG to mirror more closely its *Vorlage;* c = roots, where θ′ attempts to translate all exemplars of one Hebrew root by a single Greek root; d = transliteration, where θ′ avoids the problematic translation of difficult or foreign words by transliterating; e = apparent inconsistency in the standardization process of θ′. We also include additional commentary on several of the readings in each of the columns indicated by numerical superscripts with the corresponding notes found in the pages immediately following the charts.

4QDanᵇ	4QDanᵃ	M	o′	967	θ′	θ′ Commentary
		בשנת שלוש	ετους τριτου	=	εν ετει τριτω	b
		למלכות	βασιλευοντος	=	της βασιλειας	b
	הזון המלך הזון	בלאשצר המלך הזון	βαλτασαρ	=	βαλτασαρ¹ του βασιλεως	ae
	חזון תחלה ב..²	הזון	ορασιν³	=	ορασις	b
	אלי אני דניאל	אלי אני	την ειδον	=	ωφθη προς με	abc
		אני	εγω	=	=	=
	דניאל	דניאל	Δανιηλ	=	=	=
אחרי		אחרי	μετα	=	=	=
דניאל		הנראה	το ιδειν⁴	=	την οφθεισαν	c
		אלי	με	=	μοι⁵	b
בתחלה		בתחלה	την πρωτην	=	την αρχην⁶	c

8:1

8:2

4QDanᵇ	4QDanᵃ	M	o'	967	θ'	θ' Commentary
	ואראה	ואראה	και ειδον	και ιδου[7]	—[8]	e
	בחזון	בחזון	εν τω οραματι[9]	=	—	e
	ויהי	ויהי	—[10]	—	—	e
	בראתי	בראתי	του ενυπνιου μου[11]	=	—	e
	ואני	ואני	ειμου οντος	=	και ηλιμ	b
	בשושן	בשושן	εν Σουσοις	=	=	=
	הבירה	הבירה	τη πολει[12]	=	τη βαρει	d
אשר	אשר	אשר	קירה	—	η[13]	c
בעילם	בעילם	במדינת	εστιν εν χωρα	εστην εν χωρα	εστιν εν χωρα	d
הבירה		עילם	Ελυμαιδι	ελυμαιδει	Αιλαμ[14]	e
אשר	ואראה בחזון	—	—	—[15]	e

4QDanᵇ	4QDanᵃ	M	ο'	967	θ'	θ' Commentary
־]	־]		ετι	=	και	c
אבר דנייאל	אבר דנייאל	אבר דנייאל	ουσος μου	=	ηγην[16]	ab
	עיני	על	προς[17]	=	επι	c
	אבל	אובל	τη πυλη[18]	=	του Ουβαλ	d
ואל[	אובל	אובל	Ωλαμ	=	—	e
8:3						
ואשאאו	ואשאו	ואשאו	αναβλεψας	=	και ηρα	bc
עיני	עיני	עיני			τους οφθαλμους μου	bc
		ואראה	ειδον	=	και ειδου	c
	²⁰	והנה	—[19]		και ιδου	ac
איל	אל[	איל	κριον		κριος	b
		אחד	ενα μεγαν		εις	b
אחד בעל	אחד בעל[21]	עמד	εστωτα	ε[σ]τωτα	εστηκως	b

4QDan^b	4QDan^a	M	o'	967	θ'	θ' Commentary
לפני	לפני	לפני	απεναντι	=	προ	c
	ואבל	האבל	πυλης[22]	=	του Ουβαλ	d
הי	הי	הי	και ειχε	και ειχεν	και αυτω	b
קרנים	קרנים	קרנים	κερατα	δεχα κερατα[23]	κερατα	=
קרנימו	קרנים	קרנימים		—	—[24]	e
והאחת		והאחת	υψηλα	υφ[η]λα	=	=
	והאחת	והאחת	και το εν	=	=	=
הב מן שתים		מן שתים הב	υψηλοτερον	=	=	=
והגבוהה	והגבוהה	והגבהה	και το υφηλον	=	του ετερου	b
עלה	עלה	עלה	ανεβαινε	=	=	=
באחרונה	באחרונה	באחרנה	8:4 μετα δε ταυτα[26]	ανεβενεν	ανεβαινε	=
			8:4 μετα δε ταυτα[26]	=	(8:3) επ εσχατων	abc

4QDanᵇ	4QDanᵃ	M	o'	967	θ'	θ' Commentary
8:4						
		ואראה את	ειδον	=	=	=
		האיל את	τον κριον	=	=	=
		מנגח	κερατιζοντα	=	=	=
	ימה	ימה²⁷	προς ανατολας	προς τας ανατολας	κατα θαλασσαν	bc
	[וצפונה]	וצפנה	και προς βορραν	και δυσμας και βορραν		=
	וצפונה	וצפנה	και προς δυσμας	βορραν	και βορραν	a
[ונגבה]	ונגבה	ונגבה	και μεσημβριαν	=	και νοτον	c
ולכ	לכל	לכל	και παντα	=	και παντα	=
חיות	חיות	חיות	τα θηρια	=	=	=

4QDanb	4QDana	M	o'	967	θ'	θ' Commentary
לא	לא	לא	ουχ	=	ου	=
		יעמדו	εστησαν[28]	=	στησονται	b
		לפניו	ενωπιον αυτου	οπισω αυτου[29]	ενωπιον αυτου	=
		ואין	και ουχ ην	=	=	=
		לעזר	ο βοηθησων[30]	=	ο εξαιρουμενος	c
	וביד	מידו	εκ των χειρων αυτου	=	εκ χειρος αυτου	b
	ויעמל	ויעמל	και εποιει	=	και εποιησε	b
	כ-	כ-	ως	=	κατα	c
	[כרצנ]	כרצנ	ηθελε	ηθελεν	το θελημα αυτου	b
ויגדל	ויתגדל	ויתגדל	και υψωθη	=	και εμεγαλυνθη	c

4QDan^b	4QDan^a	M	o'	967	θ'	θ' Commentary
ואני	ואני	ואני	και εγω	=	και εγω	=
הי[י]תי	הייתי	הייתי	διενοουμην		ημην	b
		מבין		=	συνιων[31]	c
		והנה	και ιδου	=	=	=
		צפיר	τραγος	=	=	=
		העזים	αιγων	=	=	=
		בא	ηρχετο	=	=	=
	אז	מן	απο	=	=	=
	מן	המערב	δυσμων	=	λιβος[32]	c
	המערב[33]	על	επι	=	=	=
	פני	פני	προσωπου	=	=	=
	כל	כל	—[34]		πασης	b

8:5

4QDanb	4QDana	M	o'	967	θ'	θ' Commentary
[וא]רן	וארן	וארן	חד ינק	=	=	=
וא[ן	וין	וין	και ουχ	=	και ουχ ην[35]	b
	בבלע	בבלע	οαπεστο	απεστρεψεν	b
	באמד	באמד	חד ינק	=	חד ינק	=
		ולקראני	και ινκ τον τραχου	και ινκ τον τραχους	και ινκ το τραχυ	b
		קרן	χεραρ	=	χεραρ	=
		נמזח	εν	=	—[36]	=
		בל	ανα μεσον	=	ανα μεσον	=
		עיניו	των οφθαλμων αυτου	των οφθαλμων	των οφθαλμων[37]	e
		ויבא	και ηλθεν	=	=	c
8:6		עד	επι[38]	=	εως	=

4QDanᵇ	4QDanᵃ	M	o′	967	θ′	θ′ Commentary
האר[יל		האריל	του κριου	=	του κριου	b
בעל הקרנים		בעל הקרנים	τον τα κερατα εχοντα	=	του τα κερατα εχοντα	b
		ואמר	ου		ου	b
		ראיתיו	ειδον	=	=	=
		עמד	εστωτα	=	εστωτος	b
		לפני	προς	=	ενωπιον	c
		האבל	τη πυλη	εν³⁹	του Ουβαλ	d
		ויגח	και εδραμε	=	και εδραμε	=
		אליו	προς αυτον	επ αυτον⁴⁰	προς αυτον	=
		באחבת	εν θυμω	=	εν ορμη	c
בכח		בכח	οργης⁴¹	=	της ισχυος αυτου⁴¹	bc

4QDan^b	4QDan^a	M	ο'	967	θ'	θ' Commentary
וראיתיהו		וראיתיו	και ειδον αυτον	=	=	=
בובו		בובו	προσαγοντα	=	φθανοντα[42]	c
		אצלם⁴³	προς	=	εως	c
		לאיל	τον χριον	=	τον χριον	b
		להתמרמר	και εθυμωθη	=	και εξηγριανθη[44]	c
		אליו	επ αυτον	=	προς αυτον	c
		לו	και επαταξε	=	και επαιοσε[45]	c
		לאיל ואת	—⁴⁶		τον χριον	b
		וישבר	και συνετριψε	=	συνετριψεν	=
		את	τα	=	=	=
קרניו		שתי	δυο	=	αμφοτερα[47]	c
קרניו		קרניו	κερατα αυτου	=	τα κερατα αυτου	=

8:7

4QDan^b	4QDan^a	M	o'	967	θ'	θ' Commentary
		לא	και ουχετι	=	και ουχ	c
		היה	ην	=	=	=
		עם	ισχυς	εν τω χριω	ισχυς	a
		לאים	εν τω χριω	ισχυς[48]	εν τω χριω	a
		לעמד	στηναι	=	του στηναι	b
		לפניו	κατεναντι του τραγου[49]	=	ενωπιον αυτου	bc
		ויתגלבהו	και εσπαραξεν[50] αυτου	και ερραξεν αυτον	και ερριψεν αυτον[51]	c
		ארצה	επι την γην	=	επι την γην	=
		וירמסהו	και συνετριψεν[52] αυτον	=	και συνεπατησεν[53] αυτον	c
		ולא	και ουχ	=	=	=
		היה	ην	=	=	=
ולאןמצל[54]	אלה	למציל	ο ρυομενος[55]	=	ο εξαιρουμενος	c

4QDan^b	4QDan^a	M	o'	967	θ'	θ' Commentary
		לאיל	τον κριον	=	=	=
		מ-	απο[56]	=	εκ	c
		לד	του τραγου[57]	=	χειρος αυτου	c
		והצפיר	και ο τραγος	=	=	=
		העזים	των αιγων	=	=	=
		הגדיל	κατισχυσε[58]	κατερραξεν	εμεγαλυνθη[59]	bc
		עד	σφοδρα	=	εως[60]	bc
		וכ-	και οτε	=	και εν[61]	=
		עצמו	κατεσχυσε	κατεισχυσεν	το ισχυσαι αυτον	e
		נשברה	συνετριβη	=	=	=
		הקרן	αυτου το κερας	=	το κερας	b

8:8

4QDanᵇ	4QDanᵃ	M	o'	967	θ'	θ' Commentary
		הגדיל	το μεγα	=	=	=
		ותעלה	και ανεβη	=	=	=
		חזות	ετερα	=	–	e
		תצא	τεσσαρα κερατα⁶²	=	κερατα τεσσαρα	=
		תחתיה	κατοπισθεν αυτου	=	υποκατω αυτου	c
		לארבע	εις τους δυο ανεμους	=	=	=
		רוחות	ανατολαω	=	=	=
		השמים	του ουρανον	=	=	=
8:9						
		ומן	και εξ	=	και εκ	=
		ה			του	a
		אחת	ενος	=	=	=
		מהם	αυτων	=	=	=

4QDanᵇ	4QDanᵃ	M	o′	957	θ′	θ′ Commentary
		ויצא	ανεφυη[63]	ενεφυη	εξηλθε	c
		קרן	κερας	=	=	=
		אחת	ισχυρον	=	εν	a
		מצעירה[64]	εν	=	ισχυρον	e
		ותגדל	και κατισχυσε	κατεισχυσεν	και εμεγαλυνθη[65]	c
		יתר	και επαταξεν[66]	=	περρισσως	c
		אל	επι	=	προς	c
		הנגב	μεσημβριαν	=	τον νοτον[67]	bc
		ואל	και επι	=	—[68]	e
		המזרח	ανατολας	=	—	e
		ו	και	=	=	=
		אל	επι	=	προς	c

4QDanb	4QDana	M	o′	967	θ′	θ′ Commentary
8:10		הצבא⁶⁹	βορραν	=	την δυναμιν	bc
		השמים	και υψωθη	=	εμεγαλυνθη	c
		עד	εως	=	=	=
		צבא	των αστρων⁷⁰	=	της δυναμεως	c
		השמים	του ουρανου	=	=	=
		ותפל	και ερραχθη	=	και επεσεν⁷¹	b
		ארצה	επι την γην	=	=	=
		מן	απο	=	=	=
		הצבא	των αστρων⁷²	=	της δυναμεως	c
		ומן	και απο	=	=	=
		הכוכבים	αυτων⁷³	=	των αστρων	bc
		ותרמסם	κατεπατηθη⁷⁴	=	και συνεπατησεν αυτα	bc

Commentary on Dan 8:1-10

8:1

1. The orthography of βαλτασαρ "Baltasar" in θ′ provides a good example of an indication that θ′ is a recension of the OG and not a new independent translation of the Hebrew. Otherwise, we would expect a more exact transliteration of בלאשצר "Belshazzar."

2. The scribe of 4QDanª originally wrote דבר נגלה "a matter was revealed" perhaps influenced by the formula in Dan 10:1, crossed out the two words, and continued the same line with חזון נראה "a vision appeared" (=M).

3. The reading in 88-Syh, ορασις, "a vision" is hexaplarically drawn from θ′, whereas 967 preserves the OG.

4. The OG uses the infinitive το ιδειν plus the subject με in the accusative "I saw," characteristic of the Septuagint. θ′ reflects the syntax of M.

5. θ′ standardizes to reflect the Hebrew אלי "to me" more accurately, although the choice of μοι "to me" by θ′ more often reflects לי "to me" rather than אלי.

6. Both the OG and θ′ translate בתחלה "at the first" accurately; however, θ′ standardizes αρχη "first" for תחלה (see also θ′ in 8:1; 9:21,23). α′ also has αρχη in this reading, as it does in Hos 1:2 for תחלה; it never uses πρωτος "first" for תחלה.

8:2

7. Itacism in 967.

8. Most witnesses to θ′ omit the translation of the Hebrew from וארא ה to בראתי. Other witnesses to a secondarily expanded form of θ′ preserve revisions of the OG which conform to typical recensional processes.

9. ορασις, "vision" instead of οραμα, "vision" is the post-OG standardized translation of חזון.

10. The OG does not include an equivalent for ויהי, characteristic of the free, but accurate, translation.

11. The OG choice of του ενυπνιου μου "of my dream" freely but faithfully translates בראתי, "in my seeing" though it normally translates חלם "dream" or חזון "vision."

12. The OG designates Susa as "the city" instead of "the fortress" (in

the city). θ' revises with βαρις "large house, tower, fortress" which might at first look like transliteration, but is indeed the proper Greek equivalent of בירה "castle, palace, fortress" as is evidenced in Ezra 6:2, Neh 2:8, and Est 8:14.

13. The relative pronouns ητις and η are both equivalent readings for אשר. However, η becomes the favored standard choice for אשר in θ' and is employed even more consistently in α'. The OG was probably ητις εστιν εν χωρα ελυμαιδι "which is in the province of Elumaidi," as Ziegler judges. 967 has a complex error here; possible contributors to the error(s) include: itacism (εστιν / -την), confusion of ητις and εστιν (-την), and the sense of the reading since Daniel is speaking in the first person. θ' keeps the OG order but transliterates with αιλαμ. The transposed order of 88–Syh, ελυμαιδι χωρα, is probably due to hexaplaric activity.

14. θ' retains the OG word order.

15. Although it is possible that the OG and θ' simply omitted ואראה בחזון "and I saw in the vision," it is more plausible that this Hebrew phrase is an early addition in M and other Hebrew texts (cf. both 4QDana and 4QDanb). It is unnecessary here and repeats the first two words of this verse.

16. θ' ημην "I was" more exactly mirrors the Hebrew.

17. προς "toward" is an equivalent reading for על "upon"; though it more frequently reflects אל "toward"; θ' standardizes with επι "upon."

18. The OG πυλη "gate" reflects אבול "gate" rather than אובל "river." It is likely that the *Vorlage* of the OG either had the defective אבל (see M and 4QDana at 8:3) or had (or was interpreted as having) the metathesis אבול. It is thus readily understandable why the OG translates with πυλη and clear that this reading is due to mechanical error, not to the OG translator's attempt to alter the meaning of M. Both 88 and 967 suggest that the *Vorlage* was אילם or אולם, which later underwent corruption to אולי, at least by the time of Aquila who, according to Jerome, has *super ubal ulai*.

8:3

19. The OG omits והנה "and behold" possibly due to parablepsis (ואראה . . . והנה) or possibly because ואראה "and I saw" and והנה may be a pair of synonymous variants, only one of which properly occurs in any given text.

20. The text of 4QDana may well have not contained והנה.

21. 4QDana and 4QDanb add גדול "great" possibly influenced by the

description of the great horn (הקרן גדולה) of the he-goat, as found in 8:8 and 8:21. It is not likely that גדול is original, since all the references to the ram and its horn (8:3,4,6,7,20) have no such indication. The OG, however, probably translated faithfully a Hebrew text with this addition.

22. See 8:2 and note 18.

23. The addition of δεχα "ten" comes from either a secondary corrector of 967 or by the original scribe of 967. It is not from the OG translator.

24. It is most plausible that the OG and θ′ point to a *Vorlage* which had ולו קרנים גבהות = χαι ειχε (χαι αυτω, θ′) χερατα υψηλα "and it had great horns." θ′ changes the free translation of the OG χαι ειχε to the literal reading χαι αυτω, and would probably have added χαι τα χερατα "and the horns" if the equivalent Hebrew phrase were in the *Vorlage*. Thus we judge that והקרנים "and the horns" may be a later addition to M present by the time of Origen who adds χαι τα χερατα marked with the asterisk in the Hexapla (note the misplaced metobelus, which follows υψηλα in the Hexapla). If we note 8:3,4, 7,9,20,21, we have further evidence that קרנים or קרנים גבהות is the typical way the author referred to the beast, with the dual קרנים representing two kings (Media/Persia).

25. The comparative in the OG already includes the meaning of the Hebrew מן השנית "than the second."

26. The OG understands באחרנה "afterwards" as beginning the new verse instead of ending verse 3 (= M).

8:4

27. For detailed discussion of the texts witnessing to the directions see Chapter V.

28. o′ correctly uses the aorist for the imperfective יעמדו (from עמד, "stand") because the narrative sense is past tense, whereas θ′ predictably uses the future for the imperfective.

29. οπισω "behind" is probably a secondary error in 967.

30. Both o′ ρυομενος "rescuer" and θ′ εξαιρουμενος "deliverer" faithfully translate מציל "deliverer." θ′ alone uses εξαιρειν for the translation of נצל in Dan 8:4 and 8:7.

8:5

31. θ′ normally employs συνιειν "understand" for בין "understand." See Dan θ′ 1:17; 8:5; 8:17,23,27; 9:2,23; 10:11,12; 11:30,33,37*bis;* 12:8,10*bis.*

This contrasts with the OG which uses διανοεισθαι "to be minded" for בין, in Dan o′ 8:5,15,17,23,27; 9:2,23; 10:1*bis*, 11,12; 11:30; 12:8,10. θ′ does have διανοεισθαι for בין once (Dan 1:4), but that is its first occurrence in Daniel where the OG word is retained.

32. λιψ "southwest" is found for מערב "west" in 2 Chr 32:30 and 33:14; θ′ never uses δυσμη "west" for מערב.

33. אל "toward" is an error for על "upon" due to phonological similarity.

34. Either o′ translates freely while θ′ includes πασης "all" for a more exact equivalent, or כל "all" is a secondary addition in the Hebrew, not present in the OG *Vorlage* but now shared by M and Q and reflected by θ′.

35. For a discussion of אין = ουx εστιν "there is/are not" see Bodine, *The Greek Text of Judges,* 14–15.

36. θ′ lacks an equivalent for the Hebrew either because חזות "conspicuous" was not in the Hebrew *Vorlage* of θ′, or because it was unclear to θ′ and was thus omitted. חזות was probably in the OG *Vorlage,* but the OG translator read it as אחת "one," or because of the difficulty in translating this word, the translator paraphrased it with εν "one."

37. θ′ contains the true OG reading.

8:6

38. Either the OG *Vorlage* had על "upon" instead of עד "until" or the OG use of επι "upon" is a free but acceptable paraphrastic or less literal translation; however, θ′ chooses εως "until" as the standard translation of עד.

39. 967 witnesses that scribes may secondarily change prepositions.

40. 967 *Vorlage* had עליו "upon him" or this may be another instance of prepositional interchange.

41. The reading בחמת כחו "in the wrath of his power" appears to be an idiomatic phrase found nowhere else in the Hebrew Bible. Both o′ and θ′ translate it accurately, although θ′ is careful to add αυτου "his" for an exact translation of the suffix of כה. The θ′ choice of ορμη "rage" instead of the o′ reading, θυμω "anger," is probably an attempt at standardization, since ορμη is found in Ezek 3:14 θ′ for חמה; and α′ and σ′ also use ορμη for חמה in Gen 3:16. However, since θ′ uses θυμος for חמה/חמא in 3:19 and 11:44, it is not consistent. The choice of ισχυος "power" for כה is a clear case of θ′ standardization because ισχυος is found in a majority of cases for כה (8:7; 8:22;

8:24*bis*, 10:8*bis*, 10:16,17; 11:6,15,25), whereas θ′ reserves οργη, the OG choice, to translate קצף (2:12), חמה/חמא (3:13, 9:16), or זעם (8:19, 11:36) but never כה.

8:7

42. θ′ uses φθανειν "arrive, come" for the Hebrew נגע "arrive" in 8:7 and 12:12. θ′ uses προσαγειν "approach, come near" only once (7:13), for קרב (retaining the OG word, but changing the tense), whereas o′ does use προσαγειν again for נגע in Dan 10:10.

43. אצל "near" may be a later variant. The OG προς "toward" suggests אל or על, and θ′ εως "until" suggests עד in the respective *Vorlagen*.

44. εξηγριανθη "he became savage" is probably an example of θ′ standardization. Although this is the only time εξαγριαινειν appears in the Greek Bible, αγριανθησεται "to become provoked/angry" appears in 11:11 for מרר "become bitter" where the OG has οργισθησεται "become angry."

45. The choice of θ′, παιειν "strike," for נכה "strike" follows the majority of readings in the Greek Bible, as are found in Exod 12:13, Num 22:28, Josh 20:9, Judg 14:19, 1 Sam 13:4, 2 Sam 6:7, 14:6, 14:7, 20:10; 1 Kgs 16:16; 2 Kgs 9:15, 25:21; Job 2:7, 16:11; Isa 14:29; Jer 5:6, 14:19, 37(30):14; Lam 3:30. πατασσειν "strike," here the OG choice for נכה, is found twice in θ′ (2:34,35) but only for the Aramaic מחא "smite," never for נכה.

46. The OG lacks the repetitious τον κριον "the ram," which could be an expansion in M, and retains a more fluid Greek sentence mirroring the sense of M without any change in meaning.

47. αμφοτερα "both" is a θ′ revision. o′ never uses αμφοτερα, θ′ makes a distinction between שנים when it means simply "two" and when it means "both." For the first meaning, we find δυο "two" used in 5:31; 9:25,26; 12:5. αμφοτερα is found here and in 11:27 where שנים means "both."

48. 967 reflects the original OG word order, whereas 88 has hexaplarically transposed on the basis of M and θ′.

49. The OG repeats του τραγου "the goat" to clarify the antecedent. It is important to note that the OG makes this minor alteration in order to bring out the meaning of the text and not to change that meaning for its own purposes.

50. σπαρασσειν "to tear, rend in pieces" is used only three times in the Greek Bible (2 Sam 22:8 for נעע "shake," Jer 4:9 for המה "growl," and Dan 8:7), each time corresponding to a different Hebrew word. 967 ρασσειν

"strike, smite" is an early revision of the OG, also found in Dan 8:11 o′, θ′ for שלך "cast down."

51. θ′ chose ριπτειν "throw" for שלך also in 8:12. α′ also uses ριπτειν for שלך (1 Kgs 14:9, 2 Kgs 23:12, Jonah 2:4, Zech 11:13*bis*, Jer 43 [36]:23).

52. συντριβειν "break, wear out" is usually used for שבר "break" in Dan o′ (2:42) [Aram תבר], 8:7,8,22; 11:4,20,22,34), although it is also found for רמס "trample" 8:7, כשל "be thrown" 11:34, and שטף "overflow" 11:22.

53. θ′ chooses συμπατειν for רמס "trample down," as it does in 8:10,13. See Chapter V for discussion of possible theological *Tendenz* on the part of the OG translator.

54. Note the supralinear insertion of *waw* in 4QDan^b.

55. See 8:4 and note 30.

56. απο and εx are both equivalents for מ- "from."

57. o′ gives a free translation by specifying the antecedent, in the interest of clarification.

8:8

58. The true OG, xατισχυειν "to come into one's full strength," is used often in Dan o′ for גדל as well as for עצם "be mighty," עצר "retain," חזק "be strong," and עזז "be strong." The 967 reading xατερραξεν "dash down, break into pieces" is not found elsewhere in Daniel and is a later corruption of the OG; it is used seven times in the Greek Bible for other roots: ארב "ambush," הלם "smite," טול "hurl," כפף "bend," מגר "throw," and שלך "cast down." Moreover, the meaning of xαταρασσειν does not fit the context.

59. θ′ chose μεγαλυνειν "to be/become great" as the standard for forms of גדל in the Hebrew chapters of Daniel (8:4,8,9,10,25; 11:36,37); in the Aramaic section it is used for רבה "grow great." θ′ reserves xατισχυειν for חזק "grow strong" found in 11:6,7,21,32 or for עזז "be strong" found in 11:12.

60. θ′ adds εως "until" to correspond to the Hebrew עד even though it results in awkward Greek style.

61. The Cairo Geniza and a few other manuscripts have וב- "and in" reflecting the frequent confusion of *bet* and *kap* paleographically. θ′ read וב- or misread וכ- "and like" as וב- in the *Vorlage*.

62. The existence of xερατα "horn" in both o′ and θ′ could represent an expansion in the OG retained inadvertently by θ′, or could indicate that the word was in the *Vorlage* but was lost by the time of M. o′ reads אחרית

"another" for חזות "conspicuous" and thus translates with ετερα "another." θ' finds it problematic and omits it, as it does in 8:5.

8:9

63. The OG ανεφυη "grew up" is more picturesque than θ', which consistently uses εξερχεσθαι "go out" for יצא (Dan 8:9; 9:22,23; 11:11). θ' does not use αναφυειν in Daniel.

64. The Hebrew מצעירה is problematic (for the many suggestions, see Montgomery, *A Critical and Exegetical Commentary,* 338–39). The translation in ο' and θ' suggests not a form of צעיר "little, young" but of עצום "great." With witnesses in ο', 967, and θ', it is possible that עצום does represent the original (although it is also possible that the concern of θ' with word order in this case caused the translator not to notice the sense or context).

65. θ' uses forms of μεγα to correspond to the Semitic גדל "bright." See above, note 59.

66. It is possible that the OG could have read ותך "smite" for יתר "exceedingly" or paraphrases here in conjunction with what follows in 8:10.

67. τον in θ' corresponds to the Hebrew definite article ה, although Greek style does not necessitate the article before directions. θ' also changes μεσημβριαν to νοτον for "south" in 8:4.

68. θ' omits, parablepsis ואל המזרח . . . ואל הצבי.

69. הצבי "beauty" is a problematic word that each Greek translation interprets differently. ο' reads הצפון or הצפן (= βορραν, north) for הצבי. The similarities between *bêt* and *pê* and between *wāw/yôd* and final *nûn* in Herodian script make this suggestion probable. θ' reads הצבא "the army/host" for הצבי (see צבא = δυναμις "power," a few words later in 8:10). α' as well uses δυναμις for צבא in Isa 4:2, Jer 3:15.

8:10

70. The OG translates the meaning of the Hebrew. θ' mechanically substitutes one of the standard equivalents for צבא "army/host." Cf. 8:9, 10*bis,*13; 10:1, and note 69 above. θ' uses αστηρ or αστρον "star" for כוכב only (αστρον later in 8:10; αστηρ in 12:3); it is never used in Dan θ' for צבא.

71. θ' uses ρασσειν "strike" only once, in 8:11 for שלך. To translate נפל "fall" it uses the standard πιπτειν "fall," as it does eleven times in Daniel. See below, note 74, for the significance of the OG's verb ρασσειν in the passive.

72. See note 70 above.

73. The OG paraphrases with αυτων though there is no change in meaning.

74. Although the OG reading καταπατειν "trample under foot" conveys the sense of רמס, θ′ standardizes the verb συμπατειν "trample under foot" to correspond to the Hebrew רמסו (see also 8:7,13).

The problem with the OG verbs ερραχθη (note 72, above) and κατεπατηθη vis-à-vis the Hebrew text is their voice and conjugation (or stem). Both Greek verbs are in the aorist passive, whereas ותפל is a *hiphil* active imperfect and ותרמסם is a *qal* (with third person plural suffix). תפל in M is later vocalized as a *hiphil,* meaning "to cause to fall," thus the verse may be translated in English "he [the horn] caused some from the stars and (some) from the hosts to fall." But both the OG and θ′ translate it differently. The OG vocalizes תפל as a passive, (perhaps *niphal* imperfect) and uses the aorist passive ερραχθη to correspond. Thus, instead of some of the stars falling because of the action of the horn as in M, we read in the OG that the *horn* "was made to fall to the earth from the stars." Similarly, θ′ vocalized תפל differently. Instead of the *hiphil* of the MT, it is translated as a *qal,* thus the horn "fell to the earth from the hosts and from the stars." We see that in both the OG and in θ′ the horn falls, whereas in the MT the horn *causes* the hosts and stars to fall.

The second verb in question, ותרמסם, is a *qal* with the personal plural suffix. The corresponding phrase may be translated, "it [the horn] trampled them [the hosts and the stars]." θ′ translates it with the active συνεπατησεν which has the same meaning as M.

The OG, on the other hand, reads תרמם, a *niphal,* and translates it accordingly with the passive κατεπατηθη. The sense of the Hebrew is distinct, for now it (the horn) was trampled by them (the stars).

Although initially one might allege that the OG deliberately alters the text to give an earlier defeat to the horn, we find a more probable explanation to be that the OG simply vocalized an ambiguous text differently. For תפל, even θ′ preserves the same sense which the OG had, although the verbal form is distinct. Since the OG translator understood the action of תפל as affecting the horn, it was assumed that תרמם should also be translated passively.

Summary

The above analysis of 8:1–10 provides a typical sampling of the OG of Daniel 7–12. This sample contains 171 readings (judgable units). In 158, or 92.4%, the OG faithfully translates its *Vorlage,* which equals M. In 5, or 2.9%, the OG differs from M, but most likely is faithful to its own *Vorlage,* since either 4QDanᵃ, 4QDanᵇ, or θ′ agrees with G. This yields a total of 163, or 95% of the OG readings which are faithful to the *Vorlage*. Two readings, or 1.2% differ from M, and are either true omissions, or translate an alternate *Vorlage*. The different *Vorlage* is possible since the words in M, והנה and כל, which the OG "omits" are characteristic of words which are typically added to Hebrew texts. In 3 readings, or 1.7% of cases, the OG differs due to mechanical error, the cause being either from paleographical or aural confusion. An additional three readings, or 1.7% show variants in OG due to either mechanical error or variant *Vorlage*. We have not discovered any variant readings in the OG of Dan 8:1-10 which are possibly due to theological *Tendenz*.

Concerning the θ′ readings, in 69 cases, or 40% of cases, θ′ retains the OG. In 30, or 18%, the θ′ reading is dependent upon the OG. This sampling of readings confirms that θ′ is indeed a recension of the OG since a total of 58% of the readings show the OG influence on θ′. In 72, or 42%, the θ′ readings are distinct, revised in the interest of already well-known principles, that is, grammatical fidelity to M and standardization of word equivalencies.

Sample Test Cases

In order that our delineation of the OG translation technique in Daniel not be limited to one passage and in order to use a different cross-section, the following test cases for the OG translation have been selected: (1) temporal clauses, (2) roots, (3) proper names, (4) references to divinity, (5) prepositions, (6) lesser specificity, (7) greater specificity.

These examples do not purport to be exhaustive, nor do they include examples from the OG wherein the OG is so divergent from M that we suspect a different *Vorlage* (especially Daniel 4–6) or where there is extreme textual corruption (8:11–13; 9:24–27; 11:34–38). Although our study focuses upon Daniel 7–12 we include sample readings from Daniel 1–3 when they are necessary for a complete examination for the category under consideration. Moreover, these examples do not focus upon error or possible theological *Tendenz*. Rather, what we wish to show in this chapter is the way in which the OG generally proceeds to translate Hebrew and Aramaic text into readable Greek prose.

1. Temporal Clauses

The OG shows diversity in its translation of temporal clauses as shown in the following examples:

3:5

M   בעדנת די תשמעון

o′   οταν ακουσητε

θ′   η αν ωρα ακουσητε

M = o′ = θ′ "when you hear."

9:21

M   ועוד אני מדבר בתפלה

o′   και ετι λαλουντος μου εν τη προσευχη μου

θ′   και ετι εμου λαλουντος εν τη προσευχη

In this reading the OG may be reading בתפלתי "in my prayer" for בתפלה "in prayer" or μου "my" may be an insertion for clarification.

11:4

M   וכעמדו

o′   και εν τω αναστηναι αυτον

θ′   και ως αν στη

M = o′ = θ′ "and when he stood." The OG αναστηναι "stood up" reflects the OG tendency to use compound verbs.

These three examples show respectively that the OG uses relative clauses, genitive absolute plus adverb, and preposition plus infinitive to translate temporal clauses. See also 8:1 in the chart above where the genitive absolute ετους τριτου βασιλευοντος is employed for the Hebrew בשנת שלוש למלכות "in the third year of the reign."

2. Roots

Past critical studies have examined the way in which Hebrew roots are translated into Greek in order to identify the καιγε recension of various texts.[1] The purpose of the following sections on roots is not to enter into the debate concerning the θ′ text's identification with the καιγε recension, but rather to exemplify the differences in translation of Daniel OG and θ′. Whether or not Dan θ′ is καιγε, it is still an exemplar of nascent standardization of the OG. We have chosen selected root equivalences used by past examiners of Greek recensions, as well as our own.

---

[1] Past studies which developed this method include D. Barthélemy, *Les devanciers d'Aquila;* W. Bodine, *The Greek Text of Judges;* K. O'Connell,*The Theodotionic Revision of the Book of Exodus.*

עבד "work, serve"

This root occurs six times in Daniel. In Dan o' it is translated by παις "child, servant/slave" in 1:12,13; 9:6,11,17; 10:17. θ' is not consistent with his standardization, retaining the OG παις three times (1:12,13; 10:17). Moreover, θ' does revise to δουλος "slave" three times (9:6,11,17). δουλ- is the Theodotionic root for עבד in Exodus.[2]

ישר "be smooth/straight/right"

This root is identified by Bodine with ευθεια "right" as the standard equivalent by θ'.[3] ישר is used once, in Dan 11:17, where we find the expected ευθεια in Dan θ' for the OG συνθηκας "conventionally."

חזק "be/grow firm/strong, strengthen"

The evidence for the translation and recension of חזק appears to be mixed. There are twelve instances of verbal forms of this root. The OG uses ενισχυσειν "strengthen, confirm, prevail in" in 10:19; 11:5, κατισχυσειν "over-power, prevail over" in 11:7,21 and ισχυσειν "to be strong/powerful" in 10:19bis. ανδιρζου "make manly" is used once, also retained by θ' (10:19). θ' apparently revises the OG βοηθων "come to aid" (10:21) to αντεχομαι "hold against," the OG κατισχυσε to ενισχυσε, and the OG ενισχυσαι to ισχυν (11:1). In Dan 11:2 the o' text reads κατισχυσαι and θ' has κρατησαι "rule, hold sway." For this reading we suggest that the θ' reading may actually be OG and the o' text is the later recension.

חלם "dream"

Found seven times in Daniel, all instances are accurately translated. The five forms of the noun are all translated with ενυπνιον (dream, 2:1; 2:3bis; 1:7; 2:2). The two verbal forms are both used with a cognate accusative to avoid the Hebraism "to dream dreams"; thus, εμπιπτειν "fall into, occur" and ορειν "see" are found (2:1; 2:3).

חזון "vision"

The OG shows diversity in lexical choice when translating this word, but remains faithful to the meaning of the readings in M. He uses οραμα "vision" (1:17; 8:2,17,26), ορασις "vision, appearance" (8:1,15; 10:14), προφητειαν "prophetic activity/word" (11:14), and υπνω "things seen in sleep" (9:21). θ' standardizes ορασις as the consistent translation for חזון.

---

[2] O'Connell, *The Theodotionic Revision of the Book of Exodus*, 207, 295.
[3] Bodine, *The Greek Text of Judges*, 52.

גדל "grow up, become great"

The root גדל, found in M in both adjectival and verbal forms, aptly illustrates the diversity of lexical choice in the OG. The OG uses υφουν "lift high, raise up, be exalted" (8:4,10,25; 11:3,37) and κατισχυσειν (8:8,9) for the verbal forms, whereas θ′ standardizes with μεγαλυνειν "make great/powerful." For adjectival forms the OG uses ισχυρος "strong" (10:1; 11:44); μεγας "big" (8:8,21; 9:4,12; 10:4,7,8; 11:21; 12:1); and πολυς "many, much, great" (11:13,25,28). θ′ standardizes with μεγας except in 11:28 and 11:44 where πολυς is found.

We now turn to an examination of the use of a particular Greek root, καθαρος "clean, spotless."

The verbal form καθαριζειν "cleanse, purify" is used three times in o′ for three distinct roots: צדק "be just" (8:14), צרף "refine," (11:35), and לבן "make white" (11:35). θ′, however, uses καθαριζειν only once, for צדק in 8:14. This usage is most likely an instance where θ′ retains the OG, because normally we would expect καθαριζειν to be reserved for טהר "be clean, pure," as it is in approximately seventy places in the Greek Bible. It should also be considered that צדק is a later corruption of the original H צרף, for which καθαρος is a more appropriate equivalent.

The nominal form καθαρισμος "cleansing, purification" is found in Dan 12:6 where there is no Hebrew equivalent in M. This appears to be an addition for clarification.

The adjectival form καθαρος is found in o′ 7:9 for נקא "clean, pure." It is used in θ′ 2:32 for טב "good" but in the sense of "pure" gold where "good (αγαθος = the standard equivalent for טב) gold" would be awkward, and in 7:9 for נקא.

We see from this sampling that when the OG encounters a Hebrew root, there is much greater diversity in equivalencies than would be found in later recensions. However, the OG still presents an accurate rendering of the Semitic *Vorlage*. Similarly, the root of a Greek word is not limited to translating the same Hebrew root in all instances. This observation cautions us to respect the OG translator's freedom and diversity in the translation as being part of style and not *necessarily* an indication of theological *Tendenz*.

3. Proper Names

We find that the OG most frequently translates proper names exactly as found in M (= θ′). For example:

1:1

M נבוכדנאצר מלך בבל

o' ναβουχοδονοσορ βασιλευς βαβυλωνος
θ' ναβουχοδονοσορ βασιλευς βαβυλωνος

M = o' = θ' "Nebuchadnezzar/Nabuchodonosor king of Babylon."

Frequently, the OG translation of proper names is equivalent to M (and θ'), but the declension or the grammatical part of speech may vary because of syntax. For example:

1:4

M ולשון כשדים

o' και διαλεκτον χαλδαικην
θ' και γλωσσαν χαλδαιων

M = θ' "and the language of the Chaldeans." The o' reading is equivalent to M "and the Chaldean language." Sometimes the OG's translation is equivalent to M, yet θ' makes minor changes in Greek style, syntax, or use of the article to mirror M. For example,

2:13

M ובעו דניאל

o' εζητηθη δε ο δανιηλ
θ' εζητησαν   δανιηλ

M = θ' "and they sought Daniel." The o' reading is equivalent "and Daniel was sought."

2:46

M באדין מלכא נבוכדנצר

o' τοτε ναβουχοδονοσορ ο βασιλευς
θ' τοτε ο βασιλευς ναβουχοδονοσορ

M = o' = θ' "then King Nebuchadnezzar/Nabuchodonosor."

8:21

M מלך יון

o' βασιλευς των ελληνων
θ' βασιλευς   ελληνων

M = o' = θ' "the King of the Greeks."

Sometimes the OG translates a difficult Hebrew/Aramaic proper name, or an unknown one, with a paraphrase, whereas θ′ transliterates. Examples include:

1:3

M   לאשפנז

o′   αβιεσδρι

θ′   ασφανεζ

Montgomery suggests that αβιεσδρι comes from the identification of אשפנז with המלצר of 11:11, which in turn evolved into this Greek form.[4] θ′ transliterates (cf. Gen 11:2).

1:2

M   ארץ שנער

o′   εις βαβυλωνα

θ′   εις γην σεννααρ

M = θ′ "to the land of Shinar." βαβυλωνα "Babylon" is an accurate sense translation of the Hebrew. θ′ transliterates.

10:4

M   חדקל

o′   τιγρης

θ′   εδδεχελ

τιγρης "Tigris" is a correct Greek equivalent of the Hebrew חדקל (see also τιγρις in Gen 2:14). θ′ prefers once again to transliterate.

Sometimes the OG inserts nouns in apposition to the proper noun or adjectival phrase for clarification. It is also possible, however, that these additions may have been present in the *Vorlage*. For example:

1:18

M   לפני נבכדנצר

o′   προς τον βασιλεα ναβουχοδονοσορ

θ′   εναντιον   ναβουχοδονοσορ

M = θ′ "before Nebuchadnezzar/Nabuchodonosor." o′ is equivalent "before King Nabuchodonosor."

9:7

M   ולכל ישראל

o′   παντι τω λαω ισραηλ

θ′   παντι   ισραηλ

M = θ′ "and to all Israel." o′ is equivalent "and to all the people of Israel."

---

[4] Montgomery, *A Critical and Exegetical Commentary,* 124, 134.

4. References to Divinity

An examination of the OG translation of the references to the God of Israel as well as to foreign gods proves to be an interesting test case. The OG translator shows a preference to use κυριος to refer to the God of Israel, even when the *Vorlage* contains אלה/אלוהים "God."

1:17

M   האלהים

o'   ο κυριος

θ'   ο θεος

M = θ' "God" whereas o' uses the equivalent, "Lord."

2:18

M   אלה שמיא

o'   του κυριου του υψιστου

θ'   του θεου του ουρανου

M = θ' "God of heaven." o' is equivalent "Lord Most High."

Similarly, the OG will use both κυριος and θεος for a reading which has אלההון/אלוהים.

3:28 (95)

M   אלההון

o'   κυριος ο θεος

θ'   ο θεος

M = θ' "God." The o' reading is equivalent "Lord God."

10:12

M   לפני אלהיך

o'   εναντιον κυριου του θεου σου

θ'   εναντιον του θεου σου

M = θ' "before your God." The o' reading is equivalent "before the Lord your God."

The OG is not consistent in inserting κυριος, however, since we do find on occasion the use of θεος alone when referring to the God of Israel when the *Vorlage* has אלה/אלוהים. For example:

2:28

M   אלה בשמיא

o′   θεος εν ουρανω

θ′   θεος εν ουρανω

M = o′ = θ′ "God in heaven." See also 2:44.

To translate a form of אלה when it refers to a foreign god the OG often substitutes an alternate phrase:

3:18

M   לאלהיך

o′   τω ειδωλω

θ′   τοις θεοις

M = θ′ "to your gods." o′ is equivalent "to your idol" but reads a singular *Vorlage*. See also 3:12; 5:4,23.

This example might be used as an illustration of theological *Tendenz* since it could be argued that the OG wants to avoid giving any credibility to a foreign god, and uses the deprecating term ειδωλον instead of the more accurate θεος. Although the Greek Bible preserves no other instance of ειδωλον being used for אלה, it is found for אליה in Num 25:2*bis;* 1 Sam 17:43; 1 Kgs 11:2,8,33; and Isa 37:19. Thus, the OG translator of Daniel is not the first to make the equation of אליה/אלה with ειδωλον. Moreover, the translator does not totally avoid the term θεος for אלי to refer to foreign gods. For example:

3:14

M   לאלהי

o′   τοις θεοις μου

θ′   τοις θεοις μου

M = o′ = θ′ "to my gods." See also 11:36 and 11:37.

For our final reference to divinity we note that the OG also uses δεσποτης "Lord" for אדני (9:17), אליהינו (9:17), and האלה (1:17).

5. Prepositions

In investigating the prepositions עם "with," לפני "before," ־ל "to," and עד "until," we find that the OG evidences a lack of standardization in translation. In listing the following data we are cognizant of the fact that there is a problem in determining the Hebrew *Vorlage*. It may be the case that the

OG (or θ′) may not be translating the same preposition which is now present in M. This caution stated, we proceed to examine the use of these pronouns in Daniel 7-12 only because of the more readily apparent problems in determining the *Vorlage* in Daniel 1-6.

עם is found 17 times in M and is translated by the OG 13 times with μετα "with" (8:18; 9:22; 10:7,11,15,17,19,20,21; 11:8,11,17,39); once by the genitive case (7:2), once by προς "to" (7:21); once by επι "upon" (7:13); and once by the dative case of the pronoun (11:40). Thus, the OG usually translates עם with μετα though due to *Vorlage* or due to sense or context it occasionally translates with another, more appropriate preposition.

In contrast, when translating עם, θ′ uses μετα 15 times (7:13,21; 8:18; 9:22; 10:7,15,17,19,20,21; 11:11,8,17,39,40) and προς once (10:11); there is one omission, in 7:21.

The preposition לפני "before, in the presence of" is found 8 times, translated in o′ by εναντιον "before" 3 times (9:20; 10:12; 11:16); ενωπιον "before" two times (8:4; 9:18); κατεναντι "before" once (8:7); απεναντι "before" once (8:3); and προς "at" once (8:6). θ′ uses εναντιον three times (9:18,20; 10:12), ενωπιον three times (8:4,6,7), προ "before" once (8:3) and κατα "in the presence of" once (11:16).

The preposition -ל "to, toward" is found four times, translated in o′ by επι "upon, toward" (7:5 and 9:1), κατα "according to" (9:13), and εις "toward" (11:25). θ′ uses εις once (7:5), επι once (9:1), καθως "according to" once, and there is one omission (11:25).

The preposition עד "until" is found 19 times, translated in o′ 11 times by εως "until" (8:10,13,14; 9:26,27; 10:3; 11:35,36; 12:1,4,9), by επι 2 times (8:6; 11:10); and once by εις (11:24). In 5 cases the preposition is avoided in Greek (8:8; 9:25 [where עיר is read for עד]; 11:25,45; 12:6). θ′ uses εως 14 times (8:6,8,10,13,14; 9:25; 10:3; 11:10,24,35; 12:4,9; 12:1,6). θ′ uses σφοδρα "exceedingly" once for עד מאד in 11:25 where the OG is retained, and one time uses εις (11:36).

6. Lesser Specificity

Sometimes the OG is less specific or less accurate than M because of word choice or paraphrase, wherein the words chosen are more general, and allow for greater freedom in the connotation. However, the sense of the *Vorlage* is retained.

7:12
M   ושאר חיותא העדיו שלטנהון
o′   και τους κυκλω αυτου απεστησε
θ′   και των λοιπων θηριων η αρχη μετεσταθη

The OG paraphrase και τους κυκλω αυτου is also found in 7:7.

Further examples may be found by comparing the o′ and θ′ translations in the following readings. In 7:21, M reads חזה חוית, "as I looked" = εθεωρουν, θ′. o′ has και κατενοουν "and as I was understanding." In 7:28, M reads אנה דניאל שניא רעיוני יבהלנני "as for me, Daniel, my thoughts greatly alarmed me" = εγω δανιηλ διαλογισμοι μου επι πολυ συνεταρασσον με, θ′. o′ reads εγω δανιηλ σφοδρα εκστασει περιειχομην "I, Daniel, was greatly encompassed in amazement."

In the above cited examples we see how a more literal translation into Greek could have been accomplished if we look to θ′. The OG retains the sense of the Semitic text, but because of its tendency to employ a larger vocabulary, more picturesque speech, or occasional paraphrase, we have examples of lesser specificity on the part of the OG translator. (For further examples, see 9:14; 10:6,21; 12:1,4). Yet we may confidently conclude that the OG translator does not have a particular agenda he is introducing into the text nor is going beyond the sense of the Semitic text itself.

7. Greater Specificity

Sometimes the OG adds words or phrases for greater clarity, for more specificity in the text, or because the sense of M has it implicitly. Furthermore, sometimes the OG will choose a word which specifically emphasizes a single connotation of the Semitic text.

Our first reading exemplifies the OG usage of a more specific word.

7:11
M   עד די קטילת חיותא
o′   και απετυμπανισθη το θηριον
θ′   εως ανηρεθη το θηριον

The OG αποτυμπανιζειν "beat or cudgel severely" is a graphic equivalent for קטל, "kill, slay" whereas θ′ provides a more literal translation. Montgomery suggests that the OG translator's word choice may indicate "a touch of malice."[5] We would suggest, however, that this is consonant with the OG's richer vocabulary; the OG uses a stronger verb to express the same result.

Sometimes the OG adds pronouns to clarify an ambiguous text. Such examples include:

7:5
M   וארו חיוה אחרי תנינה
o′ 967   και ιδου μετ αυτην αλλο θηριον
θ′   και ιδου θηριον δευτερον

The OG μετ αυτην "with him" is an addition for clarification. Note also that the OG reflects a *Vorlage* with וארו חיוה אחרי "and behold, another beast"

---

[5] Ibid., 301-3.

whereas θ′ reflects a *Vorlage* which had וארו חיוה תנינה "behold, a second beast." M apparently is a conflation of both וארו חיוה אחרי and וארו חיוה תנינה hence, וארו חיוה אחרי תנינה "behold, another beast, a second one."

9:18

M	ושמע
o′	και επακουσον μου
967	και ακουσον
θ′	και ακουσον

μου "me" is an addition in the OG; 967 preserves an early stage of the OG recension. Otherwise, M, o′ and θ′ may be translated "and hear." επακουειν and ακουειν are both used in Dan OG; here we cannot tell whether 967 or 88–Syh preserves the original. Nonetheless, the sense is not altered. (In Dan o′ επακουειν is used three times, 9:17,18,19; ακουειν over 15 times).

9:21

M	בתפלה
o′ 967	εν τη προσευχη μου
θ′	εν τη προσευχη

The OG adds the pronoun μου "my." Otherwise, the texts are equal and may be translated "in prayer." (See also 9:21, בחזון). This OG translation may, however, represent a *Vorlage* which had בתפלתי "in my prayer."

11:15

M 4QDan^a,c	ואין כח לעמד
o′	και ουκ εσται αυτω ισχυς εις το αντιστηναι αυτω
θ′	και ουκ εσται ισχυς του στηναι

Here the OG adds αυτω twice since from the sense of the Hebrew it is appropriate. M and θ′ may be translated "and there is no strength to stand." The OG reads "and there is no strength in it to stand against him."

Sometimes the OG adds words or phrases to insure the clarity or referent of a reading, such as:

10:20

M 4QDan^a	ויאמר הידעת
o′	και ειπε προς με γινωσκεις
967	και ειπεν προς με γινωσκες
θ′	και ειπεν ει οιδας

The OG or its *Vorlage* adds προς με "to me" for clarification. 967 γινωσκες is an example of variant orthography. Concerning ει "if" in the θ′ reading, perhaps θ′ read אם (a mistake based on a misreading of ויאמר) or ειπε suffered corruption in the θ′ manuscript tradition. (For further examples, see the addition of οχλος in 11:8,43).

Sometimes the OG adds expansionist phrases, such as follows.

7:8
M   בשתכל הוית בקרניא
ο′ 967   και βουλαι πολλαι εν τοις χερασιν αυτου
θ′   προσενοουν τοις χερασιν αυτου

The OG or its *Vorlage* read משתכל "considering" as a form of משכל "scheme." πολλαι "many" is a free addition in the OG or in its *Vorlage*. (For further discussion, see Chapter III).

7:8
M   ופם ממלל רברבן
ο′ 967   και στομα λαλουν μεγαλα και εποιει πολεμον προς τους αγιους
θ′   και στομα λαλουν μεγαλα

The addition in the OG, και εποιει πολεμον προς τους αγιους "and he made war against the saints" appears to come from 7:21: וקרנא דכן עבדה קרב עם קדישין "this horn made war against the saints." Noting, however, that the OG has το χερας εχεινο πολεμον συνισταμενον προς τους αγιους "this horn joined in war against the saints" and that θ′ has το χερας εχεινο εποιει πολεμον μετα των αγιων (= M), we suggest that this addition to 7:8 is a post-OG harmonization from 7:21 which precedes the hand of Origen, since 967 includes it. The choice of το χερας εχεινο εποιει πολεμον mirrors the syntax of the Hebrew more exactly, following what we know of θ′ recensional activity, and the choice of εποιει πολεμον corresponds more precisely with עבדה קרב than does πολεμον συνισταμενον. The choice of προς (instead of μετα) for עם, however, shows the retention of the OG word. We do note that the addition fits the context at hand and does not go beyond the historical or theological data available in 7:8 and 21.

7:19
M   אכלה
ο′   κατεσθιοντες παντας
θ′   εσθιον

The OG παντας "everything" appears to be an addition so that κατεσθημι "devour" may have an object. Alternatively, παντας could come from a variant *Vorlage* which read כל אכלה "devouring everything." See also παντα in 7:25.

8:19

M	באחרית הזעם
ο′ 967	επ εσχατων της οργης τοις υιοις του λαου
88–Syh	επ εσχατου την οργης τοις υιοις του λαου σου
θ′	επ εσχατων της οργης

The OG plus, τοις υιοις του λαου, "to the sons of the people" comes from the reading of 12:1 which has τους υιους του λαου σου "to the sons of your people." (Montgomery calls this a "correct exegetical plus").[6] A later hand added σου, in 8:19, thus completing the phrase as is found in 12:1, which is witnessed in 88–Syh. This addition of the OG translator only brings out the meaning of the text; it does not change the meaning. באחרית הזעם = επ εσχατων της οργης (ο′, θ′) "at the end of the indignation."

9:16

M	ועמך
ο′ 967	και ο δημος σου κυριε
θ′	και ο λαος σου

The OG reading κυριε "Lord" is an addition, a type which would be characteristic of prayer forms (see also 9:13). ועמך = και ο δημος σου = και ο λαος σου "and your people."

10:14

M 6QDan	ובאתי
ο′ 967	και ειπε μοι ηλθον
θ′	και ηλθον

Here ειπε μοι "he said to me" is an addition *ad sensum*. ובאתי, M = ο′ = θ′.

Summary

The above sampling of test cases shows that the OG focus is upon the Hebrew/Aramaic *meaning* of the *Vorlage*, and not upon any contemporary concerns apart from the material in the *Vorlage*. The OG preserves a genuine attempt to translate the sense of the Semitic narrative. θ′ revised the OG for greater conformity with the M tradition. The θ′ text shows that the OG was a faithful translation (freer, but not less accurate). θ′ never appears to have corrected or revised the OG because the OG contained an example of theological *Tendenz*.

[6] Ibid., 352.

III

MECHANICAL VARIANTS AND ERRORS
IN THE OLD GREEK

Following upon the analysis of the translation technique of the OG translator as a whole in Chapter II, where the characteristic procedures of the translation in general and the translator's attempt to give a faithful translation of the Semitic *Vorlage* are delineated, Chapters III–V present an examination of errors, inaccuracies, and differences in the Greek text wherein the sense or meaning of the Greek text diverges from that of the Hebrew text. It may be possible, as is sometimes claimed, that some of the changes in the OG translation may have been prompted by theological *Tendenz;* these will be examined in Chapters IV and V wherein we will present examples of variant readings in the OG which may possibly have been prompted by theological *Tendenz*. Our task in this chapter, however, is to present the differences in the OG text which most scholars would agree are inadvertent mechanical changes and thus obviously errors or divergent readings not caused or prompted by theological motivation on the part of the OG translator.

The present chapter is an integral part of this study because, first of all, it enables us to uncover the characteristic types of problems and thus gives us further insight into the procedures of the translation. Secondly, since our primary task is to investigate the extent of theological *Tendenz* in Daniel 7–12, we need to know what kinds of errors typically characterize the translation as a whole. If, for example, a reading in the OG seems to preserve a distinct theological rendering, we must first investigate whether it is the same kind of error that the translator makes when the result has no apparent theological, historical, or narrative significance vis-à-vis the *Vorlage* of the OG.

By comparing the Semitic text as witnessed in Q and M with the Greek texts as witnessed in o′, 967, and θ′, we attempt to isolate the instances in which there are mechanical errors in the OG, and we include the majority of these cases in this chapter. Examples which are included in later chapters as possibilities of theological *Tendenz* are not examined here, unless they present a particularly salient example of the OG error or procedure being discussed. Moreover, certain selected examples may not be included either because they are difficult to detect or because they are *prima facie* ambiguous and are to be classified elsewhere. An effort has been made, however, to list many representative examples.

Rather than examining the readings *seriatim,* we shall categorize the variants as follows: substitution of individual letters, minuses of individual letters or phrases found in M but lacking in G, and confused sentence division.

Substitution of Individual Letters

First, we will look at those errors caused by the confusion of individual letters of Hebrew or Aramaic words with other similarly-shaped letters.[1] The past three decades of Qumran research is particularly helpful here since it is now clear why various letters could have been confused, substituted, metathesized, or omitted, due to the way in which they were formed during the Second Temple period. We also know from Qumran manuscripts that the division of words is not always clear; moreover, there are words written supralinearly which could add to the translator's confusion.

The following are examples of readings in the OG text which diverge from the Masoretic text while θ′ for the most part agrees with M. In these cases, we argue that the reason for this disagreement is that the OG misread a Hebrew letter. We are aware that often it cannot be determined whether an error was actually in the *Vorlage* or only in the mind of the translator (or scribe).

7:9
M   נור דלק
o′, 967   πυρος βαδιζουσα
θ′   πυρ φλεγον

βαδιζουσα translates הלך "walk, move" rather than דלק "flame." See also Dan o′ 12:13, where βαδισον = לך. In this case *hē* and *dālet* were confused,[2] as well as final *kap* and *qōp*.[3] This OG reading has no logical intentional purpose

---

[1] The reader may consult the paleographic charts and description in F. M. Cross, "The Development of the Jewish Scripts," *The Bible and the Ancient Near East,* 170–264. See also, Tov, *The Text Critical Use of the Septuagint,* 195–208. Specific references are made to appropriate examples in Cross's work below.

[2] Cross, "The Development of the Jewish Scripts," 138 line 2; 139 line 9; 149 line 6.

[3] Ibid., 149 lines 4,5,6.

since the description of the fire remains intact, whether it "moves" (βαδιζουσα) or "burns" (דלק).

8:9

M	ותגדל יתר
o'	και κατισχυσε και επαταξεν
967	κατεισχυσεν και επαταξεν
θ'	και εμεγαλυνθη περισσως

The o' reading και επαταξεν "and he struck" would ordinarily be used to translate ויך/ותך as it does in Dan o' 8:7. If the Hebrew reading is original, then the OG και επαταξεν was used because of the translator's reading of יתר "exceedingly" as ותך. If the tail of *dālet/rēš* is at all extended, it is easily confused with final *kap*.[4] The confusion is even more readily understandable when we note that the sequence of letters, *wāw/tāw* of ותך is identical to the first two letters of the immediately preceding word, ותגדל "to be/become great."

Concerning και κατισχυσε "and he grew strong" of o' and κατεισχυσεν of 967, we note that 967 contains an inner Greek variant, the omission of και due to homoiarchton: και κατεισχυσεν. Moreover, the orthography of κατεισχυσεν is due to the characteristic itacisms of 967. Thus we find that this reading does not preserve any intentional theological changes. Whether the little horn "became exceedingly great" (M) or "grew strong and struck" (OG), the essence of the description is unchanged. Given the use of ותגדל to describe the little horn, it is not surprising that the OG made the error in understanding the letters of יתר since יתך is appropriate for the context.

8:26

M	ואתה סתם
o'	και νυν πεφραγμενον
967	και νυν πεπραγμενον
θ'	και συ σφραγισον

Here the OG reading presupposes ועתה "and now" for ואתה "and you," which either was confused already in the *Vorlage* or in the translator's mind. *'ayin* and *'ālep* were frequently confused in the late Second Temple period due to similar or indistinguishable sounds. This reading is not an intentional change, however, because the context shows why the OG translator assumed ועתה to be appropriate, and using this word does not introduce any change in meaning. See similarly 1 Sam 28:2 where M reads לכן אתה תדע "thus you shall know" and G reads ουτω νυν γνωσει = לכן עתה תדע "thus now you shall

---

4 Ibid., 138 lines 1.2.3; 139 line 8, 149 line 4.

know."[5] The angel tells Daniel that the vision has been sealed presently (ועתה), because the vision refers to a future event. Note also that 967 errs when substituting *pi* for the correct *phi,* thus reading "having passed through" instead of the correct πεφραγμενον, "having been sealed."

9:2

M	לחרבות ירושלם
o′ 967	ονειδισμου ιερουσαλημ
θ′	ερημωσεως ιερουσαλημ

Since ονειδισμου is the normal equivalent in the OG for חרף ("reproach," Dan o′ 9:16, 11:18*bis,* and 12:2), we may posit that the *bêt* of לחרבות "desolation" was confused with *pēh.*[6] It is difficult to decide whether לחרפות or לחרבות represents the original H, since both readings are appropriate for the context. The reading in M, לחרבות, however, is nowhere else used in Daniel whereas חרפה is found four times (9:2; 9:16; 11:18; 12:2). In any case, even if the variant reading happened at the OG stage, there is no change in meaning. Whether one speaks of the "reproach of Jerusalem" or the "desolations of Jerusalem," the reference to the defilement of Jewish tradition by the presence of Antiochus remains.

10:8

M 4QDan^c	והודי נהפך
o′	και ιδου πνευμα επεστραφη
967	και ιδον πνευμα αποστραφεν
θ′	και η δοξα μου μετεστραφη

επιστρεφειν "turn about," αποστρεφειν "turn back," and μεταστρεφειν "turn oneself about," all accurately translate הפך "turn." Hatch and Redpath list several substitutions of αποστρεφειν in Codex Vaticanus (B) and επιστρεφειν of Codex Alexandrinus (A). In this reading the aorist passive επεστραφη accurately mirrors the *niphal* נהפך. The form αποστραφεν appears to be a corruption of απεστραφην. The θ′ text substitutes μεταστρεφειν here, but not in 10:16, where it retains επιστρεφειν.

Concerning והודי "and my splendor/majesty," the OG apparently understood והנה רוח "and behold, spirit" in the *Vorlage,* hence και ιδου πνευμα. 967 ιδον is a later inner-Greek error, confusion of *upsilon* and *nu.* והודי and והנה רוח could easily have been confused given the paleography.

---

[5] Tov, *The Text Critical Use of the Septuagint,* 201.

[6] If this is a paleographical error, examples would include Cross, "The Development of the Jewish Scripts," 137 line 5, 149 line 1. As Tov suggests, however, confusion of *bêt* and *pēh* could be due to phonetic similarity. See *The Text Critical Use of the Septuagint,* 202.

The confusion of *nûn* and *wāw*,[7] *rēš* and *dālet*,[8] and *wāw* and *yôd*[9] led to the error. Given the meaning of the following phrase ולא עצרתי כח "I did not retain any strength," the reading רוח = πνευμα enables the translator to keep the meaning of these phrases intact. If this is an intentional insertion by the OG translator, it is simply to bring out the meaning of the text as it was understood, not to alter the meaning for a new theological nuance or position.

10:17
M 4QDanᵃ   ואני מעתה
o'   και εγω ησθενησα
θ'   και εγω απο του νυν

The OG ησθενησα "was weak" was used because the OG read מערתי "I shook" for מעתה "from now" = απο του νυν, θ'. The OG of Daniel also uses ασθενειν for חלה "to be weak" in the *niphal* in 8:27; however we do find ασθενειν for מעד in Pss 17(18):36 and 25(26):1. θ' standardizes ασθενειν for כשל "stumble" in the *niphal* (see Dan θ' 11:14,19,33,34,35,41). This reading is plausible since the *hē* of מעתה could appear indistinguishable from a *dālet-wāw* combination.[10] A simple metathesis of *dālet* and *tāw* would yield the OG understanding, מערתי. Given the context, this reading is understandable. Daniel describes how he has no strength and no breath; ασθενειν is appropriate and does not change the import of the reading.

10:21
M   אבל אניד לך עת הרשום
o'   και μαλα υποδειξω σοι τα πρωτα
967   και μαλα και δειξαι μοι τα πρωτα
θ'   αλλ η αναγγελω σοι το εντεταγμενον

The OG τα πρωτα "the first things," results from the OG reading of הרשנ(י)ם for הרשום "the inscribed things," due to the confusion of *wāw* and *nûn*.[11] The OG και μαλα "and indeed" is an accurate translation of אבל "verily/but" (see 2 Sam 14:5, 1 Kgs 1:43, and 1 Kgs 4:14). 967 και δειξαι μοι "and to show me" is an example of an inner Greek corruption. The θ' revisions are stereotyped equivalents for θ'. See Dan θ' 2:2; 9:23; 10:21; 11:2 where

[7] Cross, "The Development of the Jewish Scripts," 137 lines 1,2; 138 line 3; 139 lines 7,9.
[8] Ibid., 137 lines 1,4,5 et al.
[9] Ibid., 137 lines 1,4,5 et al.
[10] Ibid., 137 lines 1,2 et al.
[11] Montgomery, *A Critical and Exegetical Commentary*, 418.

αναγγελειν "tell, proclaim" is used for נגד "tell" and Dan θ' 5:24,25; 10:21 where εντασσειν "arrange, order" is used for רשם "inscribe, note." Whether we read with M "but I will tell you that which is inscribed (in the book of truth)," or with the OG "but I will show you the first things (in the book of truth)," no significant change in meaning is evidenced.

11:4
M	ולאחרים מלבד אלה
o' 967	και ετερους διδαξει ταυτα
θ'	και ετεροις εκτος τουτων

In this instance the OG διδαξει "he will teach" is translating מלמד "teaching" instead of מלבד "beside"; here we see an example of confusion between *bêt* and *mēm*.[12]

11:10
M	ובא בוא
o'	και εισελευσεται κατ αυτην
θ'	και ελευσεται ερχομενος

The OG κατ αυτην translates בה "near/in it," either found in the *Vorlage,* or error due to phonological similarity. The Syriac reflects the equivalent of בו, thus showing the confusing nature of this reading.[13] The M reading is obviously corrupt. Whatever reading was original H, the OG is not engaging in *Tendenz,* but is either translating accurately or making sense out of a corrupt parent text. The meaning is not changed since κατ αυτην simply refers back to συναγωγην "a gathering" of v 10, βασιλειαν "kingdom" of v 9 or to γην "land" in v 9. The battle is still being waged by the forces of the King of the North against the King of the South (or the land of the King of the South).

11:10
M	עד מעזה
o' 967	επι πολυ
θ'	εως της ισχυος αυτου

Montgomery suggests that επι πολυ is due to the OG reading עד מאד "for a long time" for עד מעזה "as far as his stronghold."[14] Noting the Cairo manuscript reading, על מאד, על מעזה may have been in the translator's *Vorlage,* or the reading was interpreted as such. It is plausible that על and עד could

---

[12] Ibid., 426. See also, Cross, "Development of the Jewish Scripts," 137 line 3; 138 line 5.
[13] Montgomery, *A Critical and Exegetical Commentary,* 436.
[14] Ibid., 437.

be confused paleographically since if only the top stroke of the *lāmed* were missing, the remaining stroke would appear as a *dālet*. We note that in Dan 5:6, 4QDanᵃ reads חלצה for the M reading חרצה due to the confusion of *lāmed* and *rēš/dālet*. Thus, although we are acquainted with no examples of *lāmed/dālet* confusion, surely if *lāmed* and *rēš* are confused, it is virtually certain that *lāmed/dālet* could be confused. Whether the battle is waged for "a long time" or "as far as his stronghold," the OG is not altering the implications of the text.

11:12
M   והפיל רבאות
o′ 967   και ταραξει πολλους
θ′   και καταβαλει μυριαδας

ταραξει results from the OG misreading of בה(י)ל "dismay" for הפ(י)ל "cause to fall."[15] ταρρασσειν "throw into disarray" is found in the OG at 7:15 and was standardized as the θ′ and α′ correspondence for בהל as well as in other parts of the Greek Bible for בהל, but never for הפל. Whether the King of the South "casts down" (M) the opponents or "throws into disarray" (G) the army, the intention of the Hebrew text remains.[16]

11:27
M   ושניהם המלכים לכבם
o′   και δυο βασιλεις μονοι
θ′   και αμφοτεροι οι βασιλεις αι καρδιαι

The OG reading μονοι is due to reading לבדם "alone," for לכבם "their hearts," confusion of *dālet* and *bêt*.[17] The θ′ text revised δυο "two" to αμφοτεροι "two/both" for the Hebrew שנים "two" here and in 8:7 yet retains it in 5:31; 9:25,26; and 12:5. αμφοτεροι is also found for שנים in α′ in Deut 22:22 and Prov 29:13, although δυο is more frequent. Because of the confusion of the OG, the reference to the minds of the two kings being bent on mischief is not included. However, the OG does not significantly alter the meaning of the verse since these kings still ψευδολογησουσι "tell lies" (11:27).

11:45
M   ויטע אהלי אפדנו
o′   και στησει αυτου την   σκηνην τοτε
967   και στησει αυτου την τιμην σκηνην τοτε
θ′   και πηξει την σκηνην αυτου εφαδανω

[15] Ibid.
[16] See discussion below in Chapter V.
[17] Montgomery, *A Critical and Exegetical Commentary*, 454.

The original Hebrew had אהלו "his tent," = o', θ'. The present M reading, אהלי, "my tent" is a later corruption due to the confusion of *wāw* and *yôd*.[18] The original OG is found in o'. The 967 plus, τιμην "honor" is a later addition; since τιμη normally translates יקר in Dan o' (2:37; 4:27; 7:14) it is apparent that the error arises at the level of the Greek scribal tradition, probably a corruption of σκηνην "tent." The Hebrew אפדנו, a loan-word from the Persian *apadana* "palace,"[19] was problematic for the OG who read it as אדין, hence τοτε "then." Montgomery suggests that the OG is reading either אדין or אפו "then."[20] τοτε is used thirty times for אדין or באדין in Dan o'; אפו does not occur in Daniel. In light of the OG translator's pattern of making difficult words make sense in context, this reading is not surprising. The θ' text, however, transliterates אפדנו as is characteristic of this text, hence εφαδανω.

Concerning ויטע, the OG uses the more general ιστημι "set, place" for נטע, "plant." (See also Isa 51:16). θ' uses the more precise and standardized πηγνυμι "fix, plant" as does Num 24:6.

12:1

M	יעמד מיכאל
o'	παρελευσεται μιχαηλ
θ'	αναστησεται μιχαηλ

The OG reads יעבר "pass over, go on" for יעמד "stand" and translates it with παρερχεσθαι "come forward" as was done in 11:10, thus showing confusion of both *mēm/bêt* and *rēš/dālet*.[21] Whether Michael will "stand" (M) or "come forward" (G), the meaning of the text remains.

12:3

M	ומצדיקי הרבים
o'	και οι κατισχοντες τους λογους μου
967	και οι κατισχυοντες τους λογους μου
θ'	και απο των δικαιων των πολλων

Montgomery suggests that the OG is reading ומחזקי דברי[22] "and those who are strong [faithful] to my word" which may be prompted by oral confusion.

---

[18] Ibid., 468. Montgomery reports that one manuscript of Kennicott has אהלו.

[19] Ibid., 467.

[20] Ibid., 468.

[21] See above at 10:8. It is interesting to note that this same confusion occurs in 2 Sam 19:40 where the manuscripts O and ᴬL have ειστηχει = עמד, whereas M reads עבר. See Barthélemy, *Les Devanciers d'Aquila*, 112.

[22] Montgomery, *A Critical and Exegetical Commentary*, 473.

This OG understanding differs from the Hebrew (and those who make many just); nevertheless, the OG makes sense in the context, since both meanings are appropriate parallelisms for the preceding המשכלים "the wise" of this verse.

12:13

M   ותעמד לגרלך

o' 967   και αναστηση επι την δοξαν σου

θ'   και αναστηση εις τον κληρον σου

M reflects the original Hebrew לגרלך (*lectio difficilior*), whereas the OG reads לנדלך = επι την δοξαν σου "on/in your glory." Although at first consideration it may appear that the OG intentionally changes the text by using a word which may have important theological connotations, the change is best explained at the Hebrew level. This is merely a minor error where *dālet* and *rēš* were confused.[23] We find uses of δοξα in Dan θ' 11:20, 21, 39 where there is no special theological connotation. Moreover, we note that in this reading, the OG retains the positive sense of the Hebrew text. Where the M reading promised the faithful that they will stand "in your allotted place at the end of days," the OG reads, "in your glory at the end of days." The OG is clearly not offering a distinct theological understanding.

Summary

The above nineteen examples show how readily individual letters may be confused by the translator. In all of these cases, the nature of the readings was clearly not weighted with any consistent theological or historical significance; thus it is highly unlikely that the OG translator was attempting to alter the text for specific purposes. Rather, we have shown how the translator faithfully translated the meaning of the words found — or thought to be found — in the *Vorlage*.

Minuses of Individual Letters or Phrases Found in M but Lacking in OG

We now turn to another category of mechanical errors in the OG, the omissions. Again we emphasize that we are using "omission" as a formal category. Any word in M lacking in the OG is called an "omission," but we do not necessarily accept a priori that the Semitic word was indeed present

---

[23] See note 8 above.

in the *Vorlage* of the OG which would not necessarily be exactly equivalent to our present Masoretic text, nor that it ought to have been there, since M could have added, while OG retains the original text.

7:3

M	ואַרבע חיון רברבן סלקן	
o′	και τεσσαρα θηρια	ανεβαινον
967	—	
θ′	και τεσσαρα θηρια μεγαλα ανεβαινον	

The OG or its *Vorlage* omitted רברבן "great" through homoioteleuton חיון . . . רברבן. We need not posit that the OG translator was attempting to deprecate the beasts by omitting μεγαλα ; the other adjectives used to describe them in subsequent verses are intact. Alternatively, the OG may represent an original reading and M later added רברבן. 967 omits a line of text.

7:5

M	ולשטר חד הקמת ותלת עלעין בפמה בין שׁניה	
4QDanᵃ	ולשׁ]טר חד הקמת ותלת עלעין בפמה בין שׁניה]	
o′	και επι του ενος πλευρου εσταθη και τρια πλευρα ην εν τω στοματι αυτης	
967	και επι του ενος πλευρου εσταθη και τρια πλευρα ην εν τω σωματι αυτης	
θ′	και εις μερος εν εσταθη και τρεις πλευραι εν τω στοματι αυτης ανα μεσον των οδοντων αυτης	

בין שׁניה "between its teeth" may be a gloss on בפמה "in its mouth," added after the OG translation was completed, or OG omitted בין שׁניה, parablepsis following בפמה. 967 has σωματι "body" for στοματι "mouth," an inner Greek corruption due to similar sound and because of the sense of the reading, since σωματι is not incongruous with the thought expressed. There is no evidence of change because of theological *Tendenz* in the OG; the bear still has three ribs in its mouth in both M and G.

7:6

M	הוית וארו אחרי כנמר	
o′ 967	θηριον αλλο ωσει παρδαλιν	
θ′	και ιδου ετερον θηριον ωσει παρδαλις	

Either the OG omits וארו "and behold" through homoiarchton, ארו(ו) . . . אחרי, or alternatively, since וארו is used frequently, it could be an addition to M, followed by θ'. No change in meaning can be imputed by the addition or omission of וארו in any text.

7:6

M	ישלטן יהיב לה
o' 967	και γλωσσα εδοθη αυτω
θ'	και εξουσια εδοθη αυτη

The OG γλωσσα = לשן "tongue" is an example of omitted letter and metathesis.[24] (For a discussion of the putative theological *Tendenz* of this reading, see Chapter V.)

7:14

M	ולה יהיב שלטן ויקר ומלכו
o'	και εδοθη αυτω εξουσια
967	και εδοθη αυτω εξουσια βασιλικη
88–Syh	και εδοθη αυτω εξουσια ※ και τιμη βασιλικη ⅄
θ'	και αυτω εδοθη η αρχη και η τιμη και η βασιλεια

The presence of βασιλικη "kingly" in 967 may indicate that the metobelus of 88–Syh is misplaced and should be placed before βασιλικη. Thus we suggest that the true OG reading in this instance is και εδοθη αυτω εξουσια βασιλικη (= 967), omitting ויקר "and glory" due to homoiarchton (ומלכו . . . ויקר) and reading ומלכו as the adjective מלך (= βασιλικη).

These five examples show that the OG translator occasionally omits letters, words, or phrases when attempting to decipher an individual Hebrew or Aramaic reading. In these cases the resulting Greek translation is not an attempt to add to, delete from, or alter the meaning of the Semitic text. Rather, the resulting Greek phrase is an attempt to translate a Hebrew or Aramaic reading which the OG translator confused because of a mechanical error.

Confused Sentence Division

7:7–8

M	וקרנין עשר לה משתכל הוית בקרניא
o'	ειχε δε κερατα δεκα και βουλαι πολλαι εν τοις κερασιν αυτου
θ'	και κερατα δεκα αυτω προσενοουν τοις κερασιν αυτου

There are several variants in the OG reading of this phrase. Instead of

---

[24] Montgomery, *A Critical and Exegetical Commentary*, 295.

reading וקרנין עשר לה "and it had ten horns" at the end of the preceding phrase, the OG understands it to be the beginning of a new sentence. Concerning βουλαι "plans" the OG seems to have read משכ(י)ל "schemes" for משתכל "considering." Although συνεσις "understand" is normally used to translate משכיל and although there are no other attestations of βουλη as an equivalent of משכיל, since βουλη translates over sixteen different Hebrew words, most of which are singularly attested, it is apparent it could be used for several distinct Hebrew/Aramaic readings. The meaning of βουλη is certainly appropriate for משכל. It is not clear, however, what πολλαι "many" is translating. We suggest it is an addition, as is και, for sense. Even though the OG reads "there were many plans in his horns" instead of "and I considered the horns," it is clear from the context that the OG translator is not truly inserting any significant changes of meaning into the text.

8:3–4

M	והגבהה עלה באחרנה ראיתי את האיל
o′ 967	και το υψηλον ανεβαινε μετα δε ταυτα ειδον τον κριον
θ′	και το υψηλον ανεβαινεν επ εσχατων ειδον τον κριον

The OG reads באחרנה "last" with the phrase which follows. θ′ reads it correctly, following עלה "came up," and translates it literally with εσχατων. We do note, however, that the OG has not introduced any new levels of meaning to the text by the misplacing of this phrase.

11:38–39

M	ובאבן יקרה ובחמדות
6QDan	ובאבן יקרה ובחמדות
o′	και λιθω πολυτελει και εν επιθυμημασι
θ′	και λιθω τιμιω και εν επιθυμημασι

The OG reads ובחמדות "and in precious things" as the beginning of the next phrase, that is, as a prepositional phrase modifying ποιησει = עשה "he will make" of 11:39 (in which the *wāw* of ועשה is omitted) instead of as the prepositional phrase following יכבד "he will honor." The OG has not introduced any new information concerning Antiochus's activities.

Hebrew and Aramaic manuscripts of the Second Temple period show that divisions between words and sometimes even between letters of individual words are often lacking or confusing. Thus, it is understandable how the OG translator made these mechanical errors because of this confusion of spacing. Even if the details of the reasons above do not find agreement, we have made it clear that although these readings may show certain variations, there is no evidence of theological *Tendenz*.

Conclusion

The above categories of mechanical errors found in examples which are not of significant theological or historical weight show that errors on the part of the OG of Daniel 7–12 were indeed a frequent characteristic. Confusion of individual letters, omissions or additions of individual letters, metatheses of letters, as well as additions or omissions of text do not necessarily come from deliberate change. All the examples in this chapter show how readily mechanical errors can occur.

Given this tendency of the OG translator to err in readings which are strictly ordinary, we are now ready to examine variants in the OG text vis-à-vis M in which a distinct change of theological, historical, or political meaning may be present. It is now clear that the possibility of mechanical error must be investigated before claims of change due to theological *Tendenz* may be asserted. Surely, if mechanical errors characterize the translation as a whole, this possibility must be weighed before making the larger claim that changes are due to the distinct theology of the OG translator.

IV

POST-TRANSLATIONAL CHANGES
IN THE DEVELOPED GREEK TEXT

In Chapter III we investigated the types of errors which occur in the process of the Semitic text's translation into Greek. These are errors caused by misunderstood letters, metatheses, omitted letters and parablepsis. Yet not only do these occur in the process of translation, but they occur also in the course of recopying, or textual transmission, of the translation itself. Changes in the Greek text occur from secondary scribal additions or emendations, doublets, omissions, and misunderstood letters or corruptions. In this chapter we turn to these secondary scribal changes. This step is necessitated by our task of investigating possibilities of theological *Tendenz* on the part of the OG translator. When a comparison of the OG text with the Semitic shows an interesting or important variant, not only must we be certain that the change is not simply a mechanical error prompted by a misunderstanding of the Semitic text, or by an error in the *Vorlage* itself, but we must also investigate the possibility that the error derives from a secondary corruption of an originally accurate translation. If a word or phrase has additional historical or important theological meaning, but at the same time can be shown to come from a secondary stage in the history of the OG text, then there can be no claim that this datum is evidence of theological *Tendenz* on the part of the OG translator though it may show *Tendenz* on the part of some scribes.

In this chapter we investigate secondary changes in the OG text which are illustrative of the general types of problems the scribes encountered in their manuscripts or themselves made, as well as readings which modern commentators have claimed are significant on the level of the meaning of the text itself.

Some secondary additions are interesting from a grammatical point of view or as examples of mechanical variations but have no interpretative value. It is important to investigate these types of errors, however, in order to give a context in which to see the secondary additions and changes in the

OG translation of Daniel 7–12 as a whole. Thus, when a reading in the o′ text is present which putatively is evidence of theological *Tendenz* on the part of the OG translator, we are equipped to investigate the possibility that the alteration occurred not at the hands of the OG translator, but rather from a secondary scribal hand. Therefore, the first section of this chapter should be seen as paradigmatic examples of the types of alterations which accrue into the OG at a post-translational stage. We have organized these examples into the following categories:

A. Paradigmatic Secondary Errors

1. Additions and Doublets
2. Minuses
3. Misunderstood Letters, Confusions of Words

The second part of this chapter will investigate certain readings of possible theological weight which have been attributed by commentators to the OG translator. We will show on the contrary that they are indeed secondary (non-OG) changes or errors, and that hence the charge of theological *Tendenz*, if such is indeed present, may only be placed against a scribe or recensionist at a secondary level. The outline of these readings is listed below:

B. Secondary Errors of Possible Theological Significance

1. Dan 7:13, The Ancient of Days
2. Dan 10:1, The Dating of Cyrus's Tenure
3. Dan 11:25, The Attitude toward the Ptolemies
4. Dan 12:2, Those Who Rise

Throughout this chapter we note the readings of the θ′ text but since our focus is on the OG our argument will not be obscured by extensive discussion of θ′.

A. Paradigmatic Secondary Errors

1. Additions and Doublets

Additions in the OG textual tradition of Daniel 7 – 12 may come from the OG translator, or may actually come from a later secondary hand. The additions examined in this chapter are classified as later secondary insertions. Some of these secondary additions come from typical recensionists' activities wherein the OG's word choice, syntax, or other grammatical detail has been revised in order to bring the original OG into closer conformity to M. Other secondary additions come from a variant reading of an ambiguous Semitic text. When two translations of a single Hebrew phrase are identified, our assumption is that one reading is original to the OG and the other comes from a later hand. It is difficult to think that the OG translator would give two renderings of a single Hebrew word or phrase. A Greek doublet could come from a Hebrew or Aramaic doublet already present in the *Vorlage,* or it could come from an alternative translation which enters at the Greek transmission stage. Moreover, although it is theoretically possible that the OG translated the Semitic reading correctly and the second hand translated it incorrectly, this is not likely since we would not expect incorrect readings to be added. Rather, what we find in these doublets are either readings which the OG translated incorrectly and the secondary hand translates correctly, the latter being added to the OG without the former being removed, or they are readings in which the OG provided an accurate translation but which were subject to secondary revisions to more accurately mirror the Semitic text contemporary with the secondary revisionist. Beyond these two categories, we include formal doublets, or those Greek readings which are based on a *Vorlage* different from M. We include these readings in this chapter because they appear to be doublets, even though on closer analysis, it is revealed that they are accurately following an alternative Semitic text.

7:8

M ואלו קרן אחרי זעירה סלקת ביניהון

o′ και ιδου εν χερας ανεφυη ανα μεσον αυτων μικρον εν τοις χερασιν αυτου

88-Syh και ιδου αλλο εν χερας ανεφυη ανα μεσον αυτων μικρον εν τοις χερασιν αυτου

θ′ και ιδου κερας ετερον μικρον ανεβη

The OG translator read אחד "one" for אחרי "another"; hence εν "one" instead of the correct αλλο or ετερον "another." A later stage of transmission as attested in 88-Syh adds a correct reading for אחרי, αλλο, but neglects to excise εν. It is probable that αλλο was a marginal notation which later found its way into the text. We will see that both the incorrect but original reading and the corrected, secondary reading stand side by side in many instances. The OG plus, εν τοις χερασιν αυτου "in its horn" is repeated from the preceding phrase of 7:8 (=בקרניא) and serves to clarify the reading.

7:20

M	ואחרי די סלקת
o′	και του ενος του προσφυεντος
967	και του ενος του λαλουντος και προσφυεντος
88-Syh	και του ενος του αλλου του προσφυεντος
θ′	και του ετερου του αναβαντος

The OG ενος comes from reading אחד "one" in place of אחרי "another" (cf. above, 7:8). At a later stage a scribe corrects του ενος "the one" to του αλλου "the other," to conform with אחרי. 967, however, misread του αλλου as του λαλουντος "the one speaking," influenced from στομα λαλουν "a mouth speaking" in 7:20.

7:27

M	ומלכותה ושלטנא ורבותא די מלכות תחות כל שמיא
o′	και την βασιλειαν και την εξουσιαν και την μεγαλειοτητα αυτων [και την αρχην] πασων των υπο τον ουρανον βασιλειων
θ′	και η βασιλεια και η εξουσια και η μεγαλωσυνη των βασιλεων των υποκατω παντος του ουρανου

M preserves the original Aramaic reading. The OG reads כל "whole" with מלכות "kingdom" instead of with the correct שמיא "heaven." Our focus here, however, is on και την αρχην, which is not part of the original OG, but is rather a secondary addition. και την αρχην "and the authority" is a gloss on ושלטנא "and the dominion," perhaps originally written in the margin and later inserted into the text after μεγαλειοτητα αυτων "their greatness." αρχη is found in Dan θ′ 6:26 (27); 7:12; 7:14; 7:26; and 7:27 for שלטן; and αρχη is substituted in θ′ for the OG εξουσια "power, authority" in 7:12; 7:14; 7:26; and 7:27.

8:3

M	והאחת גבהה מן השנית
4QDanª	והאחת] גבהה מן השנית
o′ 967	και το εν υψηλοτερον
88-Syh	και το εν υψηλοτερον του ετερου
θ′	και το εν υψηλοτερον του ετερου

In this reading, του ετερου "than the other" is inserted secondarily in 88-Syh to bring the OG reading υψηλοτερον "higher" into closer conformity to M. Note that the OG reading "and the one was higher," although freer, does accurately translate the Hebrew, which reads "and the one was higher than the other."

8:11-12

M וממנו הרים התמיד והשלך מכון מקדשו וצבא

o′ και δι αυτον τα ορη τα απ αιωνος ερραχθη και εξηρθη ο τοπος αυτων
και θυσια και εθηκεν αυτην εως χαμαι [επι την γην] και ευωδωθη
και εγενηθη και το αγιον ερημωθησεται

967 και δι αυτον τα ορη τα απ αιωνος ερραχθη [και] εξηρθη ο τοπος
α[υτων] και θυσια και [εθηκεν αυ]την εως χαμαι επι [την] γην
κα[ι] ευωδωθη [και] εγενη[θ]η και το α[γιον ερη]μωθησεται

θ′ και δι αυτον θυσια ερραχθη και εγενηθη και κατευοδωθη αυτω και το
αγιον ερημωθησεται

Of these verses Montgomery states that they "constitute *crescendo* the most
difficult short passage of the b[oo]k."[1] We suggest the following plausible
explanation. This verse shows several doublets in the OG. Although Ziegler
brackets επι την γην only "upon the earth," και εξηρθη "and it was exalted" as
well as the entire phrase και θυσια και εθηκεν αυτην εως χαμαι επι την γην και
ευωδωθη και εγενηθη "and the eternal sacrifice, and he set it upon the ground
[upon the earth] and he prospered and grew" is secondary. Concerning the
original OG, και δι αυτον = וממנו "and from it," τα ορη "mountain" comes
from הרים "mountains," τα απ αιωνος = התמיד "the eternal sacrifice;" ερραχθη
"was dashed down" freely yet accurately translates והשלך "and it was cast
out," *pace* Montgomery who suggests that the OG read צלח "advance,
prosper." ο τοπος = מכון "place" with αυτων, an OG addition (from the suffix
of מקדשו), και το αγιον "and the holy place" comes from מקדשו, "his holy
place" with και an OG addition, and ερημωθησεται "it was made desolate"
which θ′ also retains, may point to a different *Vorlage* which had a form of
שמם "make desolate." All the other words can be accounted for as glosses
which are added into the OG text. εξηρθη is an inner-Greek error for ερραχθη.
For the remainder of the glosses we follow Montgomery's report.[2] και θυσια
is a gloss on τα απ αιωνος for התמיד; και εθηκεν αυτην is a gloss on και
εγενηθησαν for תנתן of v 12; εως χαμαι and επι την γην are both glosses on
ארצה of v 12 (note that both εως and επι are used to translate the locative
ה *pace* Montgomery who sees εως from על of על תמיד); και ευωδωθη is a
secondary gloss on ερραχθη for והשלך; and και εγενηθη is a secondary gloss
on και εγενηθησαν for תנתן.

This complicated verse is important since it shows the way that a series
of glosses may become part of the text itself. Even if there would be some
disagreement on the genesis of the glosses, most critics will agree that these
readings are indeed glosses and come not from the hands of the OG
translator but from more than one later tradition.

[1] Montgomery, *A Critical and Exegetical Commentary*, 335.
[2] Ibid.

8:16

M ויקרא ויאמר גבריאל הבן להלז את המראה

o′ 967 [και εκαλεσε και ειπε γαβριηλ συνετισον εκεινον την ορασιν] και
αναβοησας ο ανθρωπος ειπεν επι το προσταγμα εκεινο η ορασις (-σιν
88–Syh)

θ′ και εκαλεσε και ειπε γαβριηλ συνετισον εκεινον την ορασιν

Montgomery correctly notes that the reading και εκαλεσε και ειπε γαβριηλ
συνετισον εκεινον την ορασιν "and he said, 'Gabriel, cause that man to understand the vision'" is not original to the OG, but he mistakenly identifies it
as an interpolation from θ′.[3] Rather, as 967 attests, it is an early alternative
reading introduced to comply more accurately with the Hebrew, since the
OG originally understands גבריאל הבן להלז את המראה "Gabriel, make this
man understand the vision" as הגבר אל המלה הזאת המראה "a man toward
this word, the vision." A later scribe corrects the Greek to correspond with
the Hebrew; this correction is probably first written in the margin, and then
is later added into the text without the error being removed. Thus, θ′ does
not compose και εκαλεσε και ειπε γαβριηλ συνετισον εκεινον την ορασιν, but rather
inherits the clause from an earlier stage which 967 also reflects. The proposed
explanation is further supported by the use of συνετιζειν "understand" in the
doublet reading. συνετιζειν is also found in Dan θ′ in 9:22 and 10:14 for בין,
"understand" though Dan o′ has προσελθεν "approach, draw near" and ελθον
"come, go."

8:24

M ועצם כחו ולא בכחו

o′ και στερεωθησεται η ισχυς αυτου

88–Syh και στερεωθησεται η ισχυς αυτου και ουχ εν τη ισχυι αυτου

θ′ και κραταια η ισχυς αυτου

The phrase ולא בכחו "but not with his power" is an addition to M stemming
from 8:22 inserted sometime after the time of the θ′ recension, since θ′ and
the OG readings equal ועצם כחו "and his power is great" (see also Zech 4:6).
The phrase και ουκ εν τη ισχυι αυτου "but not with his power" is a later scribal
addition to the OG, inserted to conform the OG with the addition to the
Hebrew.

8:24–25

M ועם קדשים ועל שכלו

o′ 967 και δημον αγιων και επι τους αγιους το διανοημα αυτου

θ′ και λαον αγιων και ο ζυγος του κλοιου αυτου

---

3 Ibid., 347.

The Hebrew phrase ועל שכלו "and by his cunning" presents difficulties for
both o′ and θ′, and the entire phrase is rendered differently by both Greek
traditions. The OG reads ועם קדשים ועל קדשים שכלו "and the people of the
saints and his thought upon the saints." και δημον αγιων "and the people of
the saints" is a true OG phrase since a recensionist would likely use λαον. και
επι τους αγιους = ועל קדשים "and upon the saints" may come from a Hebrew-
based doublet for ועם קדשים "and the people of the saints," perhaps an
example of על/עם confusion, with עם understood by the OG to be vocalized
as עַם instead of עַל. το διανοημα αυτου translates שכלו "his thought." It may
be the case that all three texts are confused and that the original H is lost.
As M stands, ועל שכלו may be awkward. This expression is nowhere else
used in the Hebrew Bible. It is also difficult to trace what the original phrase
might have been since an alternative such as לפי שכלו "according to his good
sense" is also singularly attested (Prov 12:8), as is לשכל (Prov 23:9), בשכל
(1 Chr 26:14), and משכל (Job 17:4). θ′ actually has a change of meaning. It
vocalized עַל as עֹל and understood χλοιος "collar" to be an equivalent to שכל
(in the sense of "lay crosswise").[4]

10:1
M   ואמת הדבר
o′   και αληθες [το οραμα και] το προσταγμα
967   και αληθες το ορα < μα > και το προσταγμα
88-Syh   και αληθες το οραμα και το προσταγμα
θ′   και αληθινος   ο λογος

In this example, the original OG read και αληθες το προσταγμα "and the com-
mand is true." το οραμα "the vision" is a secondary reading for הדבר, later
joined to the OG text with και. In Daniel 7-12 the OG reserves οραμα to
translate חזון/חזון (7:7,13,15; 8:1,2,13,15,17,26; 9:24), חלם (7:1bis) or מראה
(8:26,27; 10:1), whereas οραμα is nowhere used in the OG for הדבר "the
word." Alternatively, το οραμα could be based on a Hebrew *Vorlage* which
read ואמת החזון והדבר "and the word and the vision are true" (see, for
example, 4QDanª 8:1).

11:13
M   והעמיד המון רב
4QDanª   [המון]ר[ב
o′   και συναξει [πολεως] συναγωγην μειζονα
967   και συναξει πολεως συναγωγην μειζονα
θ′   και αξει οχλον πολυν

There are two ways to account for the secondary insertion of πολις "city." Since πολις translates עיר "city," it may be that the OG *Vorlage* read והעמיד עיר המון רב "and he will raise a city, a multitude greater" with עיר being a doublet of עמיד (omission of *mēm* and confusion of *dālet* and *rēš*). Alternatively, the ο' text may preserve two renderings of רב "great." As Montgomery suggests, πολεως may be a mistake for πολλην, a doublet to μειζον.[5]

11:13

M	יבוא בוא בחיל נדול
ο'	και εισελευσεται εις αυτην [επ αυτον] εν οχλω πολλω
967	και εισελευσεται εις αυτην η επ αυτην εν οχλω πολλω
88-Syh	και εισελευσεται εις αυτην επ αυτον εν οχλω
θ'	επελευσεται εισοδεια εν δυναμει μεγαλη

In this reading, the OG read בוא "come" as בו "in it" and translated it with εις αυτην "in/to it." In the subsequent transmission stage the Syh gloss επ αυτον "on it" was added as is seen in 88-Syh. 967 incorporates this gloss with a slight change, namely, η επ αυτην "or on it." θ' = M.

11:27

M	ועל שלחן אחד כזב ידברו
ο'	δειπνησουσιν επι το αυτο
	[και επι μιας τραπεζης φαγονται]
	και ψευδολογησουσι
θ'	και επι τραπεζη μια ψευδη λαλησουσι

For the original H, ועל שלחן אחד "and upon one table," the Greek text displays a doublet. δειπνησουσιν επι το αυτο "they will dine together" is probably the original OG translation, with ועל שלחן understood in the sense of δειπνησουσιν "they will dine" and אחד read as יחדו = επι το αυτο "together."[6] The phrase και επι μιας τραπεζης φαγονται "and upon one table they will dine" is a early Hebraizing revision from a marginal reference, later inserted into the text proper. και επι μιας τραπεζης is equal to ועל שלחן אחד with φαγονται added for sense.

11:34

M	ונלוו עליהם רבים
ο'	και επισυναχθησονται επ αυτους πολλοι [επι πολεως και πολλοι]
θ'	και προστεθησονται προς αυτους πολλοι

---

5 Ibid., 440.
6 See also Jer 13:14 α' σ'; 30 (49): 3 α' σ'.

The OG originally read και επισυναχθησονται επ αυτους πολλοι "to them many will join themselves" which θ′ revises to προς αυτους πολλοι. The doublet επι πολεως και πολλοι appears to reflect a confused reading, namely על עיר ורבים "at a city, and many" which is probably a gloss based on a faulty Hebrew text.

11:39

M	ועשה למבצרי מעזים
ο′	ποιησει [πολεων] και εις οχυρωμα ισχυρον
θ′	και ποιησει τοις οχυρωμασι των καταφυγων

The doublet πολεων is probably based on an alternative Hebrew reading עיר (ערי) מבצרי (המבצרי) "fortified city, cities" for למבצרי "with the strongest [fortress]," a phrase found in Num 32:17,36; Josh 10:20; 19:29,35; 1 Sam 6:18; 2 Kgs 3:19; 10:2; 17:9; 18:8; Jer 4:5; 5:17; 8:14; 37:4; Ps 108:11; 2 Chr 17:19; Dan 11:15. עיר of this phrase was translated with πολεων "city." Perhaps, originally, the marginal gloss read εις πολεως οχυρας ισχυρου "to a fortified, strong city," and was not added to the text properly. Moreover, when this reading was added to the OG, the και, which was probably before ποιησει (και ποιησει = ועשה) was misplaced.

12:8

M	ואמרה אדני מה אחרית אלה
ο′	και ειπα κυριε τις η λυσις του λογου τουτου [και τινες αι παραβολαι αυται]
967	τις η λυσις των λογων και τι αι παραβολαι αυται
θ′	και ειπα κυριε τι τα εσχατα τουτων

The OG paraphrases אלה "of these things" by rendering this pronoun with the substantive του λογου τουτου "of this word." The doublet τινες αι παραβολαι αυται "and these very sayings" is an alternative translation, where αι παραβολαι "sayings" is substituted for η λυσις του λογου "the loosing of the word" and is subsequently joined to the text with και. παραβολαι is often used for משל.

12:11

M	ומעת הוסר התמיד
ο′	αφ ου αν αποσταθη η θυσια [δια παντος]
967	αφ ου ανασταθη η θυσια δια παντος
θ′	και απο καιρου παραλλαξεως του ενδελεχισμου

In Ziegler's judgment, δια παντος is a doublet.[7] Whether δια παντος truly is a doublet or not, both η θυσια "the sacrifice" and η θυσια δια παντος = התמיד, M "the eternal sacrifice." See also Lev 6:13 [20] where θυσια δια παντος = התמיד. If Ziegler is correct, a secondary scribe added (η) δια παντος in the margin to be read with η θυσια.

The above 15 examples show that all elements of the text transmitted as "o'" do not necessarily come from the OG translator. Thus, before claims concerning the putative *Tendenz* of the OG translator are made, the possibility that it comes from a secondary hand must be eliminated.

2. Minuses

Unlike our examples in Chapter III, the following omissions were not caused by a misreading (parablepsis, homoioteleuton, homoiarchton) of the Hebrew, but are rather inner-Greek errors. These errors stem from a copyist working with a Greek manuscript who omits Greek letters or words, usually from the same type of mechanical processes (as we saw in Chapter III) that are possible when a translator moves from one language to another.

7:2
M	וארו ארבע רוחי שמיא
o' 967	και ιδου οι τεσσαρες ανεμοι του ουρανου
88–Syh	και ιδου τεσσαρες ανεμοι του ουρανου
θ'	και ιδου οι τεσσαρες ανεμοι του ουρανου

88–Syh omits the article οι, parablepsis following ιδου. M = o' = θ' "and behold, the four winds of heaven."

7:28
M	ישתנון עלי
o' 967	διηνεγκεν εν εμοι
88–Syh	διηνεγκεν εμοι
θ'	ηλλοιωθη

In this instance, the OG εν is lost in 88–Syh by haplography.

8:3
M	ולו קרנים והקרנים גבהות
o'	και ειχε κερατα υψηλα
967	και ειχε δεκα κερατα υψηλα
88–Syh	και ειχε κερατα
θ'	και αυτω κερατα υψηλα.

[7] Ziegler, *Susanna, Daniel, Bel et Draco*, 17.

Here we note the reading of 88–Syh which lost υψηλα "high." Ziegler suggests that this is due to a misplaced metobelus; that is, Syh reads: και ειχε κερατα ※ και τα κερατα υψηλα ⋌ "and it had horns and the horns were high." If we transpose the metobelus to be placed before υψηλα, then Syh would read correctly as the OG, with the reading between the asterisk and metobelus of Syh, namely, και τα κερατα would reflect the equivalent of M, namely, והקרנים which the OG did not literally translate. In this instance, 967 also witnesses to the OG, although it adds δεκα "ten," from 7:7 and 7:24. Alternatively, it may be the case that והקרנים is a later addition to M since it is not reflected in θ'.

3. Misunderstood Letters, Confusion of Words

These errors, or inner Greek corruptions, are usually prompted by the mistaking of one Greek word for another similar Greek word with similar letters either differing in inflection or sometimes coming from a totally distinct root.

7:6

M	ולה גפין ארבע די עוף על גביה
o'	και πτερα τεσσαρα πετεινου επανω αυτου
967	και πτερα τεσσαρα πετειν[ ] αυτου
88–Syh	και πτερα τεσσαρα επετεινον επανω αυτου
θ'	και αυτη πτερα τεσσαρα πετεινου υπερανω αυτης.

In his reconstruction, Ziegler chooses πετεινου in spite of the witness of 88–Syh. We concur with his judgment since we posit that πετεινου "of a bird," was corrupted to the verbal form επετεινον "were flying." 967 has πετειν[which can only refer to πετεινου, and not επετεινον. We may suggest that the final *upsilon* of πετεινου in the original was mistakenly understood to be a *nu,* and therefore the scribe must have assumed that the initial *epsilon* has been mistakenly omitted; therefore, the scribe hyper-corrected πετεινον to επετεινον. θ' continues to mirror this OG although it changes the prepositional phrase επανω αυτου "above it," which follows, to υπερανω αυτης "above it."

7:8

M	ותלת מן קרניא קדמיתא אתעקרו
o'	και τρια των κερατων των πρωτων εξηρθησαν
967	και τρια των πρωτων κερατων εξηρθησαν
88–Syh	και τρια των κερατων των πρωτων εξηρανθησαν
θ'	και τρια κερατα των εμπροσθεν αυτου εξερριζωθη

The reading of 88-Syh εξηρανθησαν (from ξηραινειν – "were dried up") does not come from אתעקרו but rather from a similarly spelled Greek word, εξηρθησαν (from εξαιρειν – "were lifted up out of"), as is witnessed in 967. Clearly εξηρανθησαν is a later scribal corruption from the OG εξηρθησαν. It would be a misuse of these readings to accept εξηρανθησαν as the OG and to suggest that the OG used this verb instead of a correct translation of אתעקרו to further disparage the horns. Moreover, the context supports the reading of 967. To say, as does 88-Syh that "the three horns were dried up from the roots" is inappropriate. θ' has εξερριζωθη (from εκριζουν – "rooted out") for עקר, as does α' in Gen 49:6.

7:19

M	די הות שניה מן כלהון
o'	του διαφεροντος παντα
967	του διαφθειρ[ο]ντος παντα
88-Syh	του διαφθειροντος παντα
θ'	οτι ην διαφερον παρα παν θηριον

For this reconstructed OG text Ziegler emends the reading of 967 and 88-Syh διαφθειροντος "utterly destroying" to διαφεροντος "differing." It is possible that διαφθειροντος does make sense insofar as it refers to Alexander the Great who in fact did destroy the remaining Judaean kingdom. If διαφθειροντος were the correct OG, one might suspect that the reading is a salient example of interpretation on the part of the translator in order to emphasize the violence of the beast. However, this conclusion would be premature since an examination of Daniel 7 shows that διαφερω is the typical choice of the OG for שנא used to describe the beast (7:3,23,24,28); διαφθειρω is nowhere else used in Dan o'. For Dan θ' it is found for the Aramaic חבל (2:44; 4:20; 6:26 (27); 7:14), and for the Hebrew שחת (2:9; 8:24bis; 8:25; 9:26; 11:17). However, we concur with Ziegler that διαφεροντος is the original OG reading, and that διαφθειροντος is a secondary corruption due to the orthographic similarity of these two words.

10:5

M	ומתניו חגרים בכתם אופז
4QDanᶜ	ומת]ניו חגור בכ [
o'	και την οσφυν περιεζωσμενος βυσσινω και εκ μεσου αυτου φας
967	και την [οσ]φυν [πε]ριεζωσμενο[ς] χρυ[σι]ον και εκ μεσου αυτο[υ] φως
θ'	και η οσφυς αυτου περιεζωσμενη εν χρυσιω ωφαζ

Here 967 offers two alternatives for 88-Syh, namely χρυσιον "gold" for βυσσινω "fine linen," and φως "light" for φας "speaking." We note also that the phrase και εκ μεσου αυτου φας (φως) "and from its middle, speaking" seemingly has no equivalent Hebrew corresponding reading. We offer explanations for the correct OG as well as for its *Vorlage* which produced the plus.

First of all, *pace* Ziegler, we would read χρυσιον as the original OG, with βυσσινω a later, incorrect substitution from the preceding βυσσινα = בדים "linen" in Dan 10:5. βυσσινα is used four times in Dan o', at 10:5*bis*, 12:6 and 12:7. Except for this present usage in 88-Syh, in all other occasions it translates בד. Although χρυσιον usually translates זהב "gold," it is found in the Greek Bible for כתם in Job 28:16, 19; Cant 5:11; and Dan θ' 10:5.

Next we investigate the phrase και εκ μεσου αυτου φας. We hold that this is not an addition to the OG, but is rather based on a *Vorlage* which contained ומתכו פז "and from its middle, 'Paz'" following בכתם, a Hebrew doublet for בכתם אופז. Thus, φας was initially a transliteration of פז, and is the correct OG. This word was corrupted to φως at an early stage of scribal transmission and we may not conjecture that it is an attempt by the OG to add a distinct statement about the little horn. Other variants in the OG translation include the reading of ומתניו as an object instead of subject, and the ignoring of the third person singular suffix. Note also the error of 4QDanᶜ, חגור for חגרים. It is obvious that the reading was difficult to translate.

11:32

M	בחלקות
o'	εν κληροδοσια
88-Syh	εν σκληρω λαω
θ'	εν ολισθρημασι

κληροδοσια "possession, inheritance, distribution of land" is an infrequently used word, found only five times in the Greek Bible, in Dan 11:21, 32, and 34, for בחלקות "fine promises," Ps 77 (78):55 and Eccl 7:12 (11) for נחלה "possession, property, inheritance," and in 1 Macc 10:89 "tendrils." It is apparent that the OG understood this word in a way legitimate but distinct from that of M. Whereas M understands בחלקות in the sense of "fine promises," G understands it is the sense of "to be smooth." Thus, κληροδοσια is an approximate equivalent, which is close to this meaning of the Hebrew, and which does make this reading more understandable.

Although the phrase εν σκληρω λαω "among a stubborn people" might make sense in this reading, it would be non-sensical in Dan 11:21 and 11:34 where the other uses of κληροδοσια are employed. Moreover, this phrase is found one other time in the Greek Bible, 1 Kgs 12:13, where it translates העם קשה. Clearly, this phrase was not in the OG *Vorlage*. Thus, we find that the only plausible explanation is that κληροδοσια is original and σκληρω λαω is a later inner-Greek corruption.

These examples caution us to read the manuscripts of the OG tradition critically since they do not always preserve the OG. In Chapter III we saw that the OG does indeed err, make additions and omissions; however, not all variants can be attributed to errors on the part of the OG translator. In this chapter we have seen that some of the variants come not from the OG but from later secondary influences. After having seen these errors, it should not surprise us to find instances of Greek corruptions whose sense can bear a meaning which is a significant change vis-à-vis the Semitic or θ′ texts. The following examples to which we turn have been used by various modern interpreters of the Old Greek of Daniel as evidence of important theological *Tendenz* on the part of the OG translator.

B. *Secondary Errors of Possible Theological Significance*

1. Dan 7:13, the Ancient of Days

One of the most important verses in the OG of Daniel which has been cited as evidence of theological *Tendenz* on the part of the OG translator is 7:13. In his examination Bruce claims to have uncovered interpretative material which reveals "an astonishing statement about 'the one like a son of man'—that he appeared as (the) 'Ancient of Days.'"[8]

7:13
M   כבר אנש אתה הוה ועד עתיק יומיא מטה
              וקדמוהי הקרבוהי

o′   ως υιος ανθρωπου ηρχετο και εως παλαιου ημερων παρην και οι
       παρεστηκοτες προσηγαγον αυτον

88–Syh   ως υιος ανθρωπου ηρχετο και ως παλαιος ημερων παρην και οι
       παρεστηκοτες παρησαν αυτω

θ′   ως υιος ανθρωπου ερχομενος και εως του παλαιου των ημερων εφθασε
       και προσηχθη αυτω

It is important to note that Bruce presents as "the Septuagint version" the reading of 88–Syh (cf. the Swete edition) and not that of the text established by Ziegler in the Göttingen edition. Bruce offers two explanations to account

---

[8] F. F. Bruce, "The Oldest Greek Version of Daniel," 25.

for the reading of και ως παλαιος.[9] (1) ως is possibly used as "an adverbial conjunction of time" with the following sense: "as (when) the Ancient of Days arrived, then (και) the bystanders were present beside him" or ". . . then the bystanders presented him," depending on whether one accepts παρησαν αυτω or the Syro-Hexaplaric marginal reading of προσηγαγον αυτον. (2) ως is an ordinary conjunction yielding the "astonishing statement" of the translator — that the Son of Man appeared as the Ancient of Days. Bruce finds other evidence which points to this interpretative activity in the book of Revelation in which the description of the one like a Son of Man is modeled on the Ancient of Days. Also, in Mark's gospel, when Jesus speaks of the Son of Man coming on the clouds of heaven, he is convicted of blasphemy, perhaps, Bruce suggests, because the high priest understood that the Son of Man does come ως παλαιος ημερων and thus he knew Jesus was claiming to be the equal of God.

If Bruce's reconstruction were accurate for the OG he would indeed have the appropriate data to argue this case. In fairness to him it should be said that he does consider Ziegler's text, that he does weigh whether the "Septuagint reading" might be a corruption, and that he does consider the possibility of Christian influence. But it is difficult to avoid the overwhelming impression that these factors are not of predominant importance and that "the oldest Greek version of Daniel" probably "intended" the readings and meanings which Bruce describes. This impression is given by the title, structure, wording, and balance of his article.

It is presently our task to investigate whether Bruce has adequately distinguished between the OG translation, Origen's text, and possible scribal changes prior or subsequent to Origen. It is true that the aberrant readings would have been of particular noteworthiness to Christian exegetes; but before we conclude that it is the OG translator, and not a secondary scribe who engages in intentional theological *Tendenz* we must first subject the above texts to text-critical investigation.

Although 88-Syh has και ως παλαιος ημερων παρην, we note that Ziegler has reconstructed the OG as και εως παλαιου ημερων παρην "and he came unto an Ancient of Days." It is precisely this reconstruction with which Bruce disagrees. Ziegler notes that Tertullian, Cyprian, and Consultationes are based on OG witnesses to εως (του) παλαιου and not to ως παλαιος "as an Ancient [of Days]." Moreover, Ziegler suggests the probability that εως was corrupted to ως because of the preceding phrase ως υιος ανθρωπου "as a Son of Man." Furthermore, the immediately preceding και makes the loss of *epsilon* more understandable. Since εως was corrupted to ως, the genitive παλαιου would have been hyper-corrected to the nominative παλαιος in order

---

[9] Ibid., 25–26.

for the phrase to be grammatically "correct." Montgomery agrees that the text of Origen (which he incorrectly identifies with the OG) preserves an aberration, calling ως παλαιος an "ancient error."[10] Therefore, instead of calling ως παλαιος an example of great interpretative weight on the part of the OG translator, it should rather be seen as a secondary scribal development in the transmission history of the Greek text, probably even happening in two stages: εως > ως (inadvertent loss), then παλαιου > παλαιος (deliberate "correction").

As illustrations of the first stage, there are several similar secondary corruptions which follow this pattern in the recensional history of the OG of Daniel as well. This same type of confusion occurs in Dan 2:43 where 967 has και εως but 88-Syh reads και ως and in 4:30 (33) where 967 reads ως and 88-Syh has εως. Furthermore, we note that in 10:12 there is a loss of εν after εισηλθον, in 10:15 there is a loss of κατα, in 11:15 ου is omitted, and και is lacking in 11:21 in secondary developments to the OG.

We also note that the reading in 88-Syh text, παρησαν αυτω "were present beside him," is a secondary corruption of the original OG προσηγαγον αυτον "brought him" attested in the 88-Syh margin and in Justin. The secondary substitution of παρειμι for προσαγω was prompted by the preceding use of παρειμι (παρην). Once προσηγαγον was altered to παρησαν, the corruption of αυτον to αυτω follows from sense. Besides the examples noted above where a word with similar letters was confused for another distinct root, we note the other following examples of secondary corruptions in the OG tradition. In 7:28 the OG reading ετηρησα (τηρειν "watch over") is corrupted to εστηριξα (στηριζειν "hold fast") and in 8:26 the OG ερρεθη (ρειν "flow") is corrupted to ηυρεθη (ευρισκειν "find").

It should also be noted that the OG translation of עַד עַתִּיק יוֹמַיָּא "unto the Ancient of Days" by εως παλαιου ημερων "to an Ancient of Days," which lacks the article του to correspond with the emphatic state of יוֹמַיָּא, can in no way be interpreted as saying that the OG was intentionally lessening the import of the Ancient of Days by referring to him without the definite article. There are two reasons to support this. First, the OG does not consistently translate the construct chain which has the *nomen rectum* in the emphatic state with the article το. We illustrate with the following example.

7:2

M	לְיַמָּא רַבָּא
o' 967	εις μεγαλην θαλασσαν
88-Syh	εις την θαλασσαν την μεγαλην
θ'	εις την θαλασσαν την μεγαλην

---

[10] Montgomery, *A Critical and Exegetical Commentary*, 34.

This example is especially interesting because we see how a later recension of the OG, 88–Syh, alters εις μεγαλην θαλασσαν "a great sea" to correspond more precisely with the Aramaic "the great sea." Here is another example where 88–Syh does not preserve the OG, but is rather a later scribal correction.

Secondly, the OG was also influenced by the previous reference to an Ancient of Days in the poetic section of 7:9 where he is referred to without the article; it is simply ועתיק יומין = παλαιος ημερων (ο′ θ′). Both these examples show that the rendering εως παλαιου ημερων, without the article του is representative of typical OG translation practices.

This investigation of Dan 7:13 shows that to make a judgment about putative *Tendenz* in the OG based solely upon Origen's ο′ text without knowledge of the history of the text of Daniel constitutes a serious methodological error. It is essential first to establish critically the OG text and to inquire into the *Vorlage* of the OG. In this example, the OG translator accurately conveyed the text, but later corruptions and changes infiltrated the text, accounting for the variations now found in the text of 88–Syh. A study of the layers of textual development opens the possibilities for more clearly focused judgments concerning textual variants and for a more accurate assessment of the OG translation.

2. Dan 10:1, The Dating of Cyrus's Tenure

A previously unnoticed secondary corruption in the OG of Daniel occurs at 10:1.

10:1	
M	בשנת שלוש לכורש
ο′	εν τω ενιαυτω τω πρωτω χυρου
967	εν τω ετει τω πρωτω χυρου
θ′	εν ετει τριτω χυρου

First of all, we note that it is impossible to tell whether ενιαυτος or ετος represents the original OG since both are used throughout the OG translation of the Hebrew שנה "year."[11] Our interest concerns the accuracy of πρωτω "first" as part of the original OG. Hartman suggests that this change was made "probably based on an attempt to harmonize 10:1 with 1:21," where the text states that "Daniel continued until the first year of King

[11] H. St. J. Thackeray, *The Septuagint and Jewish Worship* (London: H. Milford, 1921) 125; P. Walters, *The Text of the Septuagint, Its Corruption and their Emendation* (ed. D. W. Gooding; London: Cambridge, 1973) 328–29.

Cyrus."[12] Similarly, Bludau points to 1:21 and sees the harmonization significant because it shows that the translator knew that Daniel was liberated
from Babylon.[13] Bludau's explanation gives us a clear example of the type
of hyper-interpretation with which critics have beset the OG of Daniel. It is
quite probable that 10:1 is simply a copyist's error of τω πρωτωι for τω τριτωι
"the third." In other words, the OG originally had τω τριτω but it was yet at
a secondary stage that a copyist incorrectly copied it with the other Greek
words τω πρωτω, which are orthographically similar. This is plausible since
we also note that πρωτω could not have derived from שלוש "third," but is
a likely error for τριτω. It should not surprise us that this same error is found
in the Vaticanus manuscript of Dan θ' 7:21. Moreover, it is incumbent upon
us to examine systematically all similar examples of dating in the Hebrew and
Greek of Daniel to see whether there are intentional patterns of change. We
will investigate such contextual matters in Chapter V.

3. Dan 11:25, The Attitude toward the Ptolemies

McCrystall claims that by the word choice of the OG in his description
of the Ptolemies one can discern that the translator avoided pejorative statements about them since he favored them over the Seleucids. We wish to
investigate whether the OG does in fact subtly introduce such sentiments
when discussing the Ptolemies.

11:25

M	ומלך הנגב יתגרה למלחמה
ο'	και ο βασιλευς αιγυπτου ερεθισθησεται εις πολεμον
967	και ο βασιλευς αιγυπτου ερεθει[σ]εται παραλογισθησεται εις πολεμον
θ'	και ο βασιλευς του νοτου συναψει πολεμον

McCrystall argues that the correct OG reading is και ο βασιλευς αιγυπτου
παραλογισθησεται εις πολεμον "and the king of Egypt will be misreckoned into
war" and suggests that the verb παραλογιζομαι "to misreckon" was deliberately chosen by the OG for גרה "stir up strife" instead of ερεθιζειν "to be
provoked" since the latter has negative connotations when it is found previously in 11:10 where, McCrystall claims, it "gives an anti-Seleucid tone to
the OG translation."[14] In this reading, the OG is sure to avoid such negativity
since it is now translating information about the Ptolemies, of whom it
speaks more positively. However, an examination of the use of ερεθιζειν and

---

[12] Hartman, *The Book of Daniel*, 262.
[13] Bludau, "Die alexandrinische Uebersetzung des Buches Daniel," 119.
[14] McCrystall, "Studies in the Old Greek Translation of Daniel," 330.

παραλογισθησεται shows that McCrystall's judgment is not the most likely explanation of these data. גרה is found twice in Dan 11:10, 25, and in both instances the OG chooses ερεθιζειν. ερεθιζειν is also found for גרה in Prov 15:18 and 28:25 α'. παραλογιζεσθαι is found in the Greek Bible for חלף "pass through, change, transgress," רמה "beguile," תלל "deceive," but never for גרה. We would suggest that παραλογισθησεται is a secondary insertion in the OG reflecting a *Vorlage* which has an insertion. Ziegler's judgment concerning the true OG is sustained.

4. Dan 12:2, Those Who Rise

One of the most interesting variants of the o' text is found in Dan 12:2. Of this verse, Bruce remarks, "in the resurrection passage in Dn xii 2 those who rise from their sleep . . . are divided into three, not two groups."[15] The texts read

12:2

M   אלה לחיי עולם ואלה לחרפות לדראון עולם

o'   οι μεν εις ζωην αιωνιον οι δε εις ονειδισμον οι δε εις διασποραν [και αισχυνην] αιωνιον

θ'   ουτοι εις ζωην αιωνιον και ουτοι εις ονειδισμον και εις αισχυνην αιωνιον

If the *Vorlage* of the OG = M, then we would expect the OG to read οι μεν εις ζωην αιωνιον οι δε εις ονειδισμον και εις αισχυνην αιωνιον "some to everlasting life and others to reproach and everlasting shame." Thus, this Semitic text does not account for the second οι δε in the o' text. If, however, we examine the following alternative position, we are able to account for the reading οι δε εις αισχυνην αιωνιον. The *Vorlage* of the OG originally was אלה לחיי עולם ואלה לדראון עולם "some to everlasting life and others to everlasting shame." Because לדראון "shame" is such an infrequently used word, found only in this instance and in Isa 66:24, the explanatory gloss לחרפות "reproach" was added, either into the margin originally, or into the text itself. A further indication that לחרפות is indeed a gloss is that, if the text is read without it, the parallelism of the verse is restored: אלה לחיי עולם ואלה לדראון עולם "some to everlasting life and some to everlasting shame." Based upon this *Vorlage,* the OG would have read οι μεν εις ζωην αιωνιον οι δε εις αισχυνην αιωνιον "some to everlasting life and some to everlasting shame." Corresponding to the gloss לחרפות of the Hebrew text, οι δε εις ονειδισμον

---

[15] Bruce, "The Oldest Greek Version of Daniel," 26.

"reproach" would have been inserted into the text. Thus, stage two of the developing OG: οι μεν εις ζωην αιωνιον οι δε εις ονειδισμον οι δε εις αισχυνην αιωνιον. It was only at a yet later stage, after the OG translation of the Hebrew that εις διασποραν "to dispersion" was inserted after οι δε and joined to αισχυνην αιωνιον with και. We should expect this type of insertion to have occurred at a later time, possibly as the result of a Christian-Jewish polemic. Thus, we would bracket διασποραν και in the ο′ text, and not και αισχυνην as does Ziegler.

Summary

The initial section of this chapter showed that secondary insertions indeed come into the OG text at a stage later than the translation itself. In the second section, where we investigated readings in which the claim has been made that the OG translator has engaged in theological *Tendenz,* we have suggested an alternative explanation. We believe that these readings preserve the same type of secondary insertions seen in the readings of our first section. To judge Origen's ο′ text without knowledge of Origen's procedures, or to assume that the modicum of manuscript evidence is to be taken uncritically, stretches beyond the data. Rather, as we have demonstrated in these examples of putative *Tendenz,* the OG translator has accurately conveyed the text, but at a later stage additions, omissions, and emendations have infiltrated the text which account for the variation in the ο′ text's meaning from M.

V

VARIANTS ILLUMINED
THROUGH CONTEXTUAL COMPARISON

In our last chapter we investigated variants in the o' text whose meaning led us to question whether the OG translator diverges from the *Vorlage,* by virtue of the translator's own theological perspective. We found that there are many variants in the o' text which do not stem from the translator's original work as a whole but come from various developments: recensions, errors, and corrections. This present chapter has a different task. We are still concerned with investigating variants to see whether any insight into the OG translator's own perspective may be gained. Yet now we turn to variants which come not from secondary changes, but from the actual OG translation. Our concern is to determine whether the "changes" which occurred at the level of translation are intentional or unintentional. This chapter examines OG variants most likely attributable to the OG translator which occur in passages which have parallels elsewhere in Daniel, dealing with topics which would be prime candidates for historical, political, or theological elaboration or embellishment, if such had indeed been the practice of the translator. Such topics include (1) the extent of the boundaries of the Persian empire, (2) the status of the One like a Son of Man in relation to God, (3) prophetic inclusiveness of foreign nations, (4) the political attitude toward the Ptolemies and Seleucids, and (5) the time of the end.

This chapter will not treat references atomistically as has been done in scholarly studies since the time of Bludau. Rather, it will view variants in comparison with the details of related passages. For example, in dealing with the time of the end, if the OG translator intentionally altered one reference the translator could be expected to make a consistent alteration in other passages dealing with the same time calculation. If this proves to be the case, one may attribute the variant to intentional change; if, however, the other passages dealing with the time of the end are faithfully translated and this particular variant can be attributed to mechanical error, as we saw in Chapter III, then the presumption should be in favor of unintentional mechanical error. Our operating presupposition is that, if a variant preserves an important example of theological *Tendenz,* the translator would be most likely to carry through that change systematically, especially in those cases where the lack of a similar change which had been wrought in another verse would contradict the translator's alleged intentional schema. It is difficult to accept the position that the translator would change one passage or time calculation and let the others stand unaltered. For example, if the OG translator dared to change one passage out of five on time calculations but allowed four others to remain unaltered the translator would at worst preclude any consistency of thought, and at best leave the readers and hearers in confusion.

The Extent of the Boundaries of the Persian Empire

Our first example investigates the reference to the ram which, in Daniel's vision, represents Persia. Our focus is on 8:4 wherein the o′ text differs from M in its listing of the directions toward which the ram charges. We will examine whether the OG text is the source of this variant, and if so, whether this variant signifies a distinct historical understanding on the part of the translator concerning Persian conquests. The o′ text lists four directions whereas M lists three. Our question is whether the OG translator independently added the fourth direction, or whether all four directions were present in the *Vorlage* and lost through parablepsis. If the fourth direction was in the Hebrew *Vorlage,* then the OG simply translated the available text. If, however, the fourth direction was not in the *Vorlage,* either the OG faithfully translated an alternate *Vorlage* which had added it, or it could have been added independently. Only in the case of an independent addition could the variant possibly be part of an agenda. In order to examine what the OG *Vorlage* of this verse was, we include new evidence from 4QDanᵃ. And in order to investigate whether the variant is of significant historical weight for the OG translator we examine other references in Daniel to the boundaries of foreign empires and to directions. The relevant verses are 8:9, where the directions toward which the little horn (which represents Antiochus Epiphanes) grows are listed, and 8:8 and 11:4 where the directions of the growth of the four conspicuous horns and of the division of the broken kingdom of Greece are found.

8:4

4QDanᵃ		מננח י[מה ומזרחה צפונה ונגבה
M	וצפונה ונגבה	מננח ימה
o′	χερατιζοντα προς μεσημβριαν	ανατολας χαι προς βορραν χαι προς δυσμας χαι
967	χερατιζοντα προς τας ανατολας χαι προς δυσμας βορραν χαι μεσημβριαν	
θ′	χερατιζοντα χατα θαλασσαν χαι βορραν χαι νοτον	

In the discussion of the Hebrew versions of 8:4, both Montgomery and Di Lella find the direction of the ram's charging to be significant indications of the author's understanding of the extent of the Persian empire. Montgomery accepts M, wherein three directions are given, as representative of the original text and claims, "Persia was the Far-Oriental empire to the Semitic world, hence the expansion only to three points of the compass is stated."[1] Di Lella states, "It is rather strange that no mention is made of the extension of the Persian empire to the east. . . . Perhaps our author was not interested in the extreme eastern part of the Persian empire because there was no Jewish Diaspora there in his time.[2] If the inclusion of only three directions in M is indeed of particular significance, then is it also true that the inclusion of a fourth in the o′ text preserves a distinct notion of Persian activities? According to Montgomery, who sees the addition of προς ανατολας as intentional OG alteration, the translator knew of further eastern lands that Persia conquered, echoing the author of Esth 1:1 who uses the expression "from India to Ethiopia." Therefore, Montgomery argues, "accordingly, G adds 'to the east.'"[3] If one were to judge the addition προς ανατολας in light of Di Lella's comments about M's lack of inclusion of it, one might argue that the addition represents a new interest on the part of the translator in the eastern empire, perhaps because the Diaspora was reaching toward that area.

In order to respond to this issue, we now turn to the questions posed in the introduction to this example.

Possibility A. Was the fourth direction present in the Hebrew *Vorlage* and the OG a simple, accurate translation of it? Since 4QDanᵃ, 967, and 88–Syh witness to the presence of מזרחה "eastward" we cannot assume that the OG translation is aberrant. It is possible that מזרחה was in the *Vorlage* of the OG. If this were the case we could account for the differences in the texts as follows: In 4QDanᵃ מזרחה is included, but is placed after ימה "westward" and before צפונה "northward" thus not exactly corresponding to any of the Greek witnesses. On the one hand, we could argue that the original Hebrew text did indeed only have three directions and 4QDanᵃ and the OG independently added the fourth direction since they were compelled to complete the list of only three directions. On the other hand, the Hebrew of 4QDanᵃ reads poetically with its placement of *wāw* before the second and fourth direction, and thus we could argue that it preserved the original. If

[1] Montgomery, *A Critical and Exegetical Commentary,* 328.
[2] Di Lella, *The Book of Daniel,* 234.
[3] Montgomery, *A Critical and Exegetical Commentary,* 328.

4QDanᵃ is indeed the oldest form of the Hebrew, then the original OG would have read, κερατιζοντα προς δυσμας και ανατολας βορραν και μεσημβριαν "charging westward and eastward, northward, and southward" (we omit the repetitions of προς according to OG style). When, at a later stage, δυσμας and ανατολας were metathesized, the προς was repeated. This is reflected in 967, namely, προς (τας) ανατολας και προς δυσμας βορραν και μεσημβριαν (τας here may be a later scribal mistake). Similarly, when at a later stage of corruption, δυσμας and βορραν were metathesized, προς and και were again repeated, yielding προς ανατολας και προς βορραν και προς δυσμας και μεσημβριαν (ο'). μεσημβριαν never has a προς added before it because it always remained in the final placement of the four directions. At a stage later than 4QDanᵃ, the Hebrew text lost מזרחה and the wāw of this word was joined to צפונה thus yielding the M reading (= θ'). Perhaps מזרחה followed מגנח "charging" at a later Hebrew development and was easily lost through parablepsis. A similar development of verses could be posited but we might also suggest that the OG followed a Hebrew *Vorlage* which included מזרחה even though this was an error, or secondary development.

Possibility B. If M and θ' would in fact preserve the most ancient version, we posit that the OG originally read κερατιζοντα προς δυσμας και βορραν και μεσημβριαν (= M). If, as is customary, the OG translator did not hold it necessary to include the wāw of וצפונה, the phrase in OG would read κερατιζοντα προς δυσμας βορραν και μεσημβριαν. If this reading is truly the OG, we could account for the omission of the και before βορραν in 967 and the use of προς before only two of the directions in 967. We suggest that this original OG was later corrupted by a secondary addition that made its way into 967 as follows. A gloss, προς τας ανατολας, was written in the margin and later, as often happens for the insertion of marginal readings, was joined with και. Thus, the first stage of the corrupted OG, namely, κερατιζοντα προς τας ανατολας και προς δυσμας βορραν και μεσημβριαν would be preserved in 967. We note that the inclusion of the distinct τας before ανατολας and not before any other direction also adds weight that ανατολας is a gloss.

The second stage of the corrupted OG is seen in the ο' text. At either Origen's stage or in some manuscript after 967 προς τας ανατολας > προς ανατολας (parablepsis, *sigma*) and the directions ανατολας, δυσμας, βορραν, and μεσημβριαν are put in orderly counter clockwise directional system, namely, ανατολας βορραν δυσμας and μεσημβριαν, with the words και and προς which preceded δυσμας in the first stage of the reconstructed OG being repeated before βορραν when δυσμας and βορραν are reversed in the second stage.

Possibility C. This argument would again presuppose that M and θ' preserve the original but that the addition of προς ανατολας is not a secondary corruption but is in fact an addition at the hands of the OG translator. The reading מזרחה in 4QDanᵃ is also an addition, but an independent one.

Evaluation. The above possibilities are only three of many ways which could be posited to account for the variations of the four texts. We do not believe that it is possible to arrive at a definitive solution for this particular variant. However, it is probable that M = θ′ preserves the original here, since a later omission of one of the four directions would be harder to account for, whereas a later inclusion of a fourth is readily understandable since if one sees three directions listed, one would expect a fourth. Thus, the rule of *lectio difficilior* would be applicable here.

The issue which is important for our concern in this chapter, however, is the intentionality of the inclusion of προς ανατολας. If possibility A is correct, and if ανατολας simply translates a *Vorlage* which had מזרחה (whether or not מזרחה is original) then obviously no *Tendenz* could be attributed to the translator. If possibility B is correct and the addition comes from a secondary corruption, then again no *Tendenz* could be attributed to the translator. If possibility C is correct then one final question remains: does the inclusion of ανατολας preserve an example of *Tendenz,* or is it simply an unwitting addition because three directions were seen and a fourth expected?

In order to answer this question we should ask: are there any other references in Daniel to the eastern extent of the Medeo-Persian empire, or are there any other times when directions are similarly mentioned?

First, we note that there are no further references to the boundaries of the Medeo-Persian empire in Daniel. Secondly, we do find that there are references to directions in 8:5,9; 11:5,6,7,8,9,11,14,15,25,29,40, and 44. Yet these examples, most of which simply refer to the king of the north and the king of the south, do not include any mention of all four directions which might shed light on any pattern of speech used when listing them in Daniel. But first we note that a further search of the Hebrew Bible outside Daniel yields no further illumination. There are seven different patterns with which to list the four directions, with only one pattern, east, west, north, south, used more than once.[4] Nevertheless, a search of Daniel does give us one relevant, illuminating verse consisting of directions used in the same manner as found in 8:4. In 8:9, the he-goat, which symbolizes Alexander, charges against the ram in three directions. In examining this verse we have two

---

[4] The seven patterns are (1) west, east, north, south, Gen 28:14, (2) east, west, north, south, 1 Chr 9:24, Ps 107:3, Isa 43:5, (3) east, north, south, west 1 Chr 26:17, (4) south, west, north, east, Num 34, (5) north, east, south, west, Ezek 48, (6) north, south, east, west, Gen 13:14 (7) north, west, south, east, 1 Kgs 7:25.

interests. Does use of directions give us any indication of how the author of Daniel employed directions, thus shedding light on whether the Hebrew of 8:4 as preserved in the MT is original or secondary? Secondly, does the OG translation of 8:9 tell us whether or not this translator was wont to change the directions of the *Vorlage* for intentional purposes?

8:9

M   ותגדל יתר אל הנגב ואל המזרח ואל הצבי

ο' 967   και κατισχυσε και επαταξεν επι μεσημβριαν και επ ανατολας και
           επι βορραν

θ'   και εμεγαλυνθη περισσως προς τον νοτον και προς την δυναμιν

The M reading הצבי "the glorious land" is original, although it caused confusion for the OG and for θ'. The OG βορραν translates הצפון "north," which was present in a faulty *Vorlage* or due to an error. θ' δυναμις = הצבא "army," as in 8:10. Dan θ' normally transliterates צבי with σαββειν, found in 11:16, 41, and 45, although in Isa 4:2, α' and θ' use δυναμις for צבי, referring to Israel. και is a later revision toward M.

In this verse we find that the author of Daniel does indeed use directions intentionally and accurately. Alexander's exploits extended to the east, to the south, and toward Israel. For the author, Alexander's empire stretches in these directions and thus is reflected in the text. In light of this we would suggest that the author of Daniel uses directions intentionally with the three directions employed in 8:4 wherein Persia spread westward, northward, and southward.

Now we may examine what the OG does in translating this reference to Alexander. We suggest that צבי is the original, as is frequently in Daniel 11, and that the OG either erred, because of mechanical error or intentionally changed the reading to הצפון = βορραν. We would reject the possibility that the OG *intentionally* changed the reading to צפון because he would then be wrong concerning an event close to his time and geography, since it is doubtful that he would have had knowledge of Alexander's conquests of the North. We would argue therefore, that the OG translator simply misread צבי as צפון in this instance especially when we note that in 11:16 and 11:45 צבי = θελησεως "will," OG. Other than the misreading of צפון for צבי, the OG translator does not alter the directions relevant to the boundaries of the empire of Alexander. He did not include an addition of "to the west," for example. Therefore, if the OG did not add additional information about the extent of Alexander's empire, we should not posit that it intentionally added additional information about events and geography about Persia, an empire more distant both in time and location. Why, then, would the OG translator add "to the east" in 8:4? We argue that this unintentional error occurred either because it was in the *Vorlage* as 4QDan^a attests, or because the translator was focusing on the language of the verse itself and not the historical boundaries referred to in the autograph. This type of inclusiveness of all directions was a common practice, as witnessed by 4QDan^a itself.

Moreover, the clue could have been received from M of Daniel itself wherein directional statements may express inclusiveness and not specificity as found in 8:8 and 11:4. In 8:8 we read that after the great horn of the he-goat is broken it is followed by four horns which grow לארבע רוחות השמים = εις τους τεσσαρας ανεμους του ουρανου "toward the four winds of heaven" (ο', θ'). Similarly, in 11:4, the kingdom of Alexander is said to be divided לארבע רוחות השמים = εις τους τεσσαρας ανεμους του ουρανου (ο', θ'). In these two instances we find that directional references may express inclusiveness and not specificity. It is also true that statements such as "the King of the North" or "the King of the South" refer to specific kings and "North" and "South" may also indicate the particular kingdoms of the Seleucids and Ptolemies. In 8:4 and 8:9 the author of Daniel uses directions to indicate the extent of the boundaries of foreign empires. However, by looking at the OG of 8:4 in light of the Hebrew *Vorlage* and in light of 8:9 we may conclude that the OG did not intentionally add προς ανατολας. Rather, it either translated a *Vorlage* which had מזרחה, or added it as a generalizing statement of inclusiveness concerning the completeness of Persia's domination over Babylon, already known from the Hebrew text itself. We may conclude that Dan 8:4 OG does not give us any information about what the OG translator knew concerning the extent of foreign empires.

The Status of the One Like a Son of Man
in Relation to God

We have previously examined 7:13 in Chapter IV concerning the description of the Son of Man; another aspect of 7:13 presently warrants investigation in this chapter, namely, the coming of the Son of Man either *with* or *on* the clouds of heaven. Our question here is whether the OG translator used επι "upon" instead of μετα "with" when translating עם "with" in order to give a distinct theological interpretation to the status of the Son of Man. Does the way in which the Son of Man is related to the clouds on his arrival hold within it a key to understanding his status as being either human or divine? We examine this issue in light of the use of the expression in Ugaritic and Hebrew phraseology, the use of Hebrew and Aramaic prepositions and their translation into Greek, an examination of the Son of Man in the context of Daniel 7. If it could be shown that coming on the clouds can only be referred to when God arrives and that coming with the clouds is a way of referring to the rider as being less than divine, and if the OG altered this human reference ("with") to a divine reference ("on") then one could claim that the OG translator does indeed engage in theological *Tendenz* by his choice of επι for עם in 7:13 when referring to the Son of Man's coming. If, however, the Greek and Hebrew expressions do not make these distinctions through prepositions, or if the OG translator typically translates Hebrew prepositions with a multiplicity of Greek equivalents, then one could not claim that the OG translator includes theological *Tendenz* in 7:13 and changes the author's portrayal of the Son of Man. Moreover, if the OG allegedly changes the interpretation of the Son of Man in 7:13 to be equal to God, one should examine the entirety of references to the Son of Man in Daniel 7 to see whether other references to the Son of Man imply divinity.

7:13

M	וארו עם ענני שמיא
o'	και ιδου επι των νεφελων του ουρανου
θ'	και ιδου μετα των νεφελων του ουρανου

Montgomery and Hartman make the claim that there is indeed theological *Tendenz* in the OG's use of επι. In his textual notes to M, Hartman maintains that it is significant that M reads "with the clouds of heaven" and not "on the clouds" for the latter "would ordinarily be said only of God; clouds accompany the human figure on its arrival."[5] Although he does not elaborate on the OG translation, the implication is that since the OG does use επι = upon/on, a shift has occurred in the interpretation of the Son of Man from being solely a human figure to including aspects of divinity. Hartman thus echoes Montgomery who comments, "position *upon* the clouds, which the writer avoids, would rather be the attribute of Deity . . . and his enthronement upon the cherubs."[6] Thus, both these authors see the way in which the Son of Man arrives to be important when we consider the relationship of the Son of Man to God.

This point is further developed by J. Lust. Lust agrees with Rahlfs's reading of 7:13 (which we examined in Chapter IV) and argues that the OG of 7:13 is based on a Hebrew, and not Aramaic, original which is theologically similar to Ezekiel's vision wherein

> Ezechiel in his vision sees God as one "in the likeness of a man" sitting on "the likeness of a throne." This must be the source of inspiration of Daniel's description of the one "like a son of man." This evidence is often discarded for the

5 Hartman, *The Book of Daniel*, 206.
6 Montgomery, *A Critical and Exegetical Commentary*, 303.

simple reason that the TM of Daniel puts the "Ancient of Days" on the throne and not the "Son of Man." However, in the Septuagint, the "Son of Man" and the "Ancient of Days" are the same. This definitely suggests that the Septuagint preserved an older textform in which the sources of Daniel's inspiration can still be discovered.[7]

For Lust, the "Septuagint" did not alter its *Vorlage* to produce a new theological insight about the Son of Man; rather, the interpretation of the divine Son of Man was originally present in a Hebrew *Vorlage* only later to be changed by the Aramaic translation of it. He holds that the Hebrew original had עַל "upon" which was later translated into Aramaic as עַם "with." He thus argues, "The Septuagint wishes to identify the 'son of man' with the 'Ancient of Days.' He is God. Therefore they present him as riding 'on the clouds,' the clouds being known as a vehicle of the gods."[8] Thus, for Lust, Dan 7:13 o′ provides an important clue for understanding the earliest view of the Son of Man in Daniel as God. The riding *on* the clouds is an important constitutive element in his understanding.

In order to respond to these claims we first examine this Aramaic phrase in the context of possible Ugaritic and Hebrew parallels. The debate on whether Daniel 7 is replete with Canaanite imagery continues. Cross notes that "the '*nny šmy*' who come with the 'one like a man' belong to the traditional entourage of Ba'l, the (deified) storm cloud (or cloud chariot) accompanying him or on which he rides."[9] Similarly, J. Collins argues that much of the imagery of Daniel 7, especially the references to the sea and its monsters, the Ancient of Days, the one like a Son of Man and the rider of the clouds, and the judgment scene and the divine assembly have their roots in the Canaanite myths of Baal and El.[10] Recently, however, A. Ferch has challenged these conclusions of Collins, arguing that the entirety of the constitutive images of the vision in Daniel 7 depart significantly from the events described in the Canaanite myths concerning the relationship between El and Baal. Nevertheless, even Ferch admits that the Son of Man shares with Baal the imagery of "Rider of the Clouds" and states, "the epithet 'Rider of the Clouds' is frequently attributed to Baal (bearing some similarity to the S[on] of M[an] coming 'on' or 'upon' the clouds of heaven)."[11] This

---

[7] J. Lust, "Daniel 7,13 and the Septuagint," *ETL* 54 (1978) 68.

[8] Ibid., 64.

[9] F. M. Cross, *Canaanite Myth and Hebrew Epic* (Cambridge: Harvard, 1973) 17. See also the earlier discussion of J. A. Emerton, "The Origin of the Son of Man Imagery," *JThS* 9 (1958) 225-42.

[10] J. Collins, *The Apocalyptic Vision of the Book of Daniel* (HSM 16; Missoula: Scholars, 1977) 96-106.

[11] A. Ferch, "Daniel 7 and Ugarit: A Reconsideration," *JBL* 99 (1980) 82.

well-known epithet of Baal, *rkb 'rpt* "rider of the clouds," does not tell us which preposition was necessary when using this phrase to refer to Deity since the construct state is used, with *rkb* governing *'rpt*.[12] This Ugaritic phrase is echoed in Ps 68:5 (4 Eng) with the Hebrew לרכב בערבות. Here neither עם nor על is used; rather, the preposition -ב is found. In Isa 19:1 God is referred to as the one who רכב על עב קל = καθηται επι νεφελης κουφης "is riding on a swift cloud," and in Isa 14:14 the King of Babylon boasts: אעלה על במתי עב אדמה לעליון "I will ascend above the heights of the clouds, I will make myself like the Most High." The cited Ugaritic phrase as well as the Hebrew examples from Ps 68:5 and Isa 19:11 show that both the Hebrew and Ugaritic use this phrase only when referring to deity and that there is no strict or consistent use of prepositions in these phrases. The example from Isa 14:14 shows that to "ascend upon the back [= riding] of the clouds" is tantamount to making oneself "like the Most High." Nevertheless, this Isaian passage (14:15) shows that the king fails since we read, אך אל שאול תורד אל ירכתי בור. Given that Dan 7:13 is the only place in the Hebrew Bible where the riding of the clouds is specifically used to refer to anyone other than God, there is not enough evidence to argue that when one speaks of the Son of Man's arrival עם must be used instead of על, -ב, or the simple participle.

But even if we presuppose that the Aramaic intentionally used עם since the author thought that על must be restricted to deity, we must recall the OG translator's ideas about the function of prepositions. As we have seen in Chapter II, one of the main characteristics of the OG translation in general is translation for accurate conveyance of sense, without standardization or meticulousness. Our investigation of the use of prepositions in Daniel 7–12 similarly has shown that the OG translator is not consistent. Although there are no other instances in the Greek texts of Daniel where ο′ reads επι and θ′ has μετα for עם there are several examples of confusion, inconsistency, or simple freedom in translation. Extensive standardization of prepositions does not come until α′, as even θ′ is not consistent, although θ′ is more consistent than ο′. The OG translator attempts to provide an accurate sense translation and does not pause to render a particular Semitic preposition with the same Greek preposition at all times. For the OG, επι is the most frequently used preposition, found for אל, על, -ב, -ל, לפני, and עד. The OG may have chosen it for עם as well, if this were indeed in the *Vorlage*.

But we need not presuppose that עם was necessarily in the OG translator's *Vorlage*. There may have been an error, or the translator could have erred in reading it. Although there are no attestations in Daniel where עם and על were confused, there are places in other books of the Hebrew

---

[12] *CTA* 5.5.6-11; 2.1.35; 10.2.33.

Bible where similar confusion occurs. For example, in Isa 36:11, 1QIsaᵃ has עַם "with" whereas M has אֶל "to."[13] Moreover, it is significant that in 2 Sam 2:5 4QSamᵃ has עַל "upon," M has עַם "with," and G employs επι "upon" which fairly consistently reflects עַל in the OG of Samuel.[14] We do indeed have examples in 4QDan where other prepositions are confused as well. In 8:5 4QDanᵃ has אֶל, where M has עַל = επι οʹ, θʹ. In 2 Sam 13:24 Q has אֶל where M has עַם, and in 1 Sam 9:18 Q has אֶל where M has אֵת.[15] In Exod 17:2 M (= SP) has עַם where the Cairo Geniza manuscript has עַל. It is clear that prepositions are prime candidates for confusion when copying manuscripts in the same language and even more so when translating. Even αʹ who consistently tried to standardize prepositions made errors. In Hos 12:14 (5) αʹ uses μετα for אֶל where αʹ thought אֶל was אֵת. Thus, we find that an important objection needs to be raised against this method of interpretation on the part of Hartman, Montgomery, and Lust. To assert that the OG translator was trying to equate the Son of Man with God by using επι instead of μετα isolates a single letter of a Hebrew/Aramaic preposition and gives it great weight without at all examining the OG's use of prepositions in the translation technique and without considering the possibility of a variant reading in the *Vorlage*.

In summary, we have found several possibilities to account for the OG's reading of επι. First, given the frequency and the freedom with which the OG translates prepositions, the translator could have chosen επι for עַם and thought that accurate sense was maintained. Secondly, given the confusion of prepositions from the copying of one Hebrew or Aramaic text to another and from Hebrew to Greek translation, we find that the OG could have found a preposition other than עַם, or misread עַד or עַל for עַם. Finally, in our response to modern interpreters who claim that the OG's choice is an example of theological *Tendenz* wherein the Son of Man is equated with God, we note that nowhere else does the OG translation hint of a divine Son of Man. In Chapter IV we have seen that the change of εως παλαιου to ως παλαιος is a secondary corruption, as Ziegler established. Indeed, an examination of the entirety of the visions of Daniel 7–12 shows that the Son of Man may represent the collectivity of the saints of the Most High or may be a leader of the saints. With either interpretation, as Collins states, "the leader represents the collective unit in any case."[16] The Son of Man, variously interpreted,

---

[13] S. Talmon, "Aspects of Textual Transmission of the Bible in the Light of Qumran Manuscripts," *Qumran and the History of the Biblical Text,* 236.

[14] Ulrich, *The Qumran Text of Samuel and Josephus,* 80.

[15] Ibid., 77 and 106.

[16] J. Collins, "The Son of Man and the Saints of the Most High in the Book of Daniel," *JBL* 93 (1974) 64.

indeed has a special status in relation to God whose dominion is everlasting and whose kingdom is indestructible (Dan 7:14) but neither for M nor for the OG is the statement ever made that he was divine.

Prophetic Inclusiveness of Foreign Nations

Through the process of translation of the Hebrew Scriptures into the Greek language one might suspect the possibility of greater inclusiveness by means of word choice. Perhaps the use of the Hebrew Bible among Greek-speaking Jews who lived in a heterogeneous culture led translators, either consciously or unconsciously, to include other peoples among those groups addressed in Scripture. In order to examine whether there is an inclusion of people other than Jews in the OG translation of Daniel we examine 9:6 wherein the prophets are said to have spoken to various groups in Israelite history. By the choice of words in the OG translation, are we able to detect any change of connotation in the referents of the groups listed? For example, if the OG used a particular Greek word to translate עַם "people" when it referred to Israel, and an alternate word to refer to nations or people other than Israel and used the more inclusive term for a Hebrew text which the author clearly intended to refer to Israel alone, then we would have an example of greater universalism on the part of the OG translator. The verse which has been singled out for a salient example of supposed greater prophetic universalism by Bruce is 9:6. If the OG translator indeed tried to show greater inclusiveness in this example, we should also investigate whether this same type of change occurred in other instances where the people Israel are addressed. The immediate context of 9:6, the prayer which Daniel addresses to God for forgiveness, has several references to Israel in the Hebrew text. Moreover, there are other references to Israel in Daniel 7 and 12. We will turn to these examples to investigate the degree of faithfulness of the OG translation when reading references to Jews after we look at 9:6 itself.

9:6

M	וְאֶל כָּל עַם הָאָרֶץ
ο′	και παντι εθνει επι της γης
θ′	και προς παντα τον λαον της γης

In Bruce's examination of the way in which וְאֶל כָּל עַם הָאָרֶץ "and to all the people of the land" is translated, he claims to have found an interpretation of the OG which signals "a note of wider universalism."[17] Of this putative

[17] F. F. Bruce, "The Oldest Greek Version of Daniel," 24.

intentional change from the Hebrew to the OG he remarks, "the prophets who spoke 'to all the people of the land' (Dan. ix 6) are now said to have spoken 'to every nation on earth.'"[18] Before we can posit any particular theological significance in the choice of εθνος "nation," we first of all examine the way in which עם is translated in Daniel 7–12. The two Greek equivalents found are εθνος "nation" and λαος "people." On the one hand, if it is the case that εθνος is used only for Israel, then Bruce would have grounds for his position. On the other hand, if both εθνος and λαος are accurate faithful translations of עם without strict distinction in connotation, then we would disagree with Bruce's analysis of the motivation behind the OG translator.

In Daniel ο' 7–12, λαος translates one Hebrew word, עם, in ten places where it refers to Israel (7:27; 9:15,19,20,24; 10:14; 11:32; 12:1*bis;* 12:7). It is also used twice to refer to Israel when the context implies עם, although this word itself is not expressed in the Hebrew (8:19; 9:7). An examination of εθνος shows that although it translates גוי "nation" in 8:22 and 11:23, it is also legitimately used for עם in 7:14; 9:6; 9:26; 11:14; 11:33.[19] What is most interesting, however, is that while εθνος refers to foreign nations (7:14; 8:22; 9:26) it also refers to Israel (11:14; 11:33). In addition, 11:23 is ambiguous, but most likely the reading does refer to Israel. We presently take special note of 11:14 and 11:32 where the references are unambiguously addressed to Israel.

11:14

M	ובני פריצי עמך
ο'	και ανοικοδομησει τα πεπτωχοτα του εθνους σου
θ'	και οι υιοι των λοιμων του λαου σου

We are focusing upon עמך "your people" in this phrase = του εθνους σου "your nation," ο' and του λαου σου, θ'. We note that because of mechanical errors the sense of the OG differs from M and θ'. ο' understands ובני "and the sons" as ובניתה, hence ανοιχοδομησει "and you will build;" and פריצי "the violent ones" as a construct, hence τα πεπτωχοτα "the fallen ones." Although the use of πιπτω is unusual for פרץ, it is found in Amos 9:11 (Hatch and Redpath err when they do not identify πεπτωχοτα with פרץ). Even though the sense of the OG differs from the Hebrew, עמך of the OG *Vorlage* refers to Israel as does the OG translation of it. We may translate και ανοιχοδομησει τα πεπτωχοτα του εθνους σου as "and he [the King of the South] will build up the

<hr>

[18] Ibid.

[19] The standardization climaxes in α' who uses εθνος thirty-eight times for גוי, once for אוה, once for לאם, perhaps once for איב (although Ziegler suggests that instead of τω εθνοι the text should be emended to τω εχθρω), and twice for עם. λαος translates עם alone in α'.

fallen ones of your people." "Your people" refers to Daniel's people, just as it does in M and θ'. εθνος in this case means exactly what λαος means in 11:14 θ'. It is not reserved for people who are not part of עם ישראל "the people of Israel" as Bruce argues.[20] In short, at the earlier stage of the OG both εθνος and λαος were options for translating עם (= Israel); in the later recensional stage λαος alone became the standardized equivalent.

Our next example of the use of εθνος in 11:33 shows once again that this Greek word may indeed translate עם = Israel in the OG of Daniel.

11:33

M ומשכילי עם יבינו לרבים

o' και εννοουμενοι του εθνους συνησουσιν εις πολλους

θ' και οι συνετοι του λαου συνησουσιν εις πολλα

Both o' and θ' are equivalent translations of the Hebrew (and those among the people who are wise shall make many understand), referring to the wise Jews who remain faithful. The OG use of εθνους for עם does not change the reference. Clearly the wise are from Israel since the context discusses the profanation of the temple and the consequent destruction of the people who are plundered.

After having seen the way in which εθνος is used in 11:14 and 11:33 we may now return to 9:6. It is possible that the phrase και παντι εθνει επι της γης does indeed refer to the Jews in this context for the OG translator, just as עם does for the Hebrew original. Thus, we examine the possible reasons for the absence of the article before εθνος. We note that if επι were not in the OG text, namely, if the OG read και παντι εθνει της γης, it would be a literal translation and an accountable reading of M. We consider possible reasons for the inclusion of επι below. Our point here is to explore whether the OG translator's failure to include the article necessarily implies that the phrase και εθνει must be understood distributively, being translated "and to every people/nation." Rather, could it be translated, "to all people" or "to all the people"? An examination of Greek grammatical principles concerning the use of πας and an examination of examples from classical Greek literature shows that not every instance of πας with a noun without the article should be taken distributively. H. Liddell and R. Scott list the following examples: πασα υλη is to be translated "all the wood," and πασα αληθειη is equivalent to "all the truth."[21] Thus, although Bruce's translation of the OG και παντι εθνει, "and to every nation" is appropriate and accurate, it is also possible to

---

[20] See also McCrystall, "Studies in the Old Greek Translation of Daniel," 92.

[21] H. G. Liddell, and R. Scott, *A Greek-English Lexicon* (rev. H. S. Jones; Oxford: Clarendon, 1940) 1345-46.

translate the phrase, "and to all the people." Therefore, we see that the omission of the article, and the usage of the term εθνος does not necesarily imply that the OG translator is referring to people other than Jews.

The presence of επι in this reading is enigmatic. It could be genuine OG and was used simply because of the general freedom that the OG employs, not necessarily because of a particular agenda. It might also be based upon a *Vorlage* which vocalized עַם as עִם and substituted עַל, or επι could be a translation of עַם as it may well have in 7:13 OG. επι could also be a secondary insertion.

One further step remains to investigate the claim of any consistent pattern of inclusiveness in the OG translation of Daniel. We now examine the immediate context of 9:6, namely the prayer of Daniel in 9:4b–19 where several references to God's past relationship with Israel and Israel's sinful response is delineated. Daniel admits that his people have not listened to all the prophets who have spoken God's word, επι τους βασιλεις ημων και δυναστας ημων και πατερας ημων και παντι εθνει επι της γης = אל מלכינו שרינו ואבתינו ואל כל עם הארץ M "to our kings, our princes, and our fathers and to all the people of the land" (9:6). In this verse several groups in Israel are listed: kings, leaders, ancestors, and all other people of Israel. The prayer continues emphasizing how Israel has transgressed God's commandments. Nothing is said to imply that God's word is spoken to other nations. Those concerned are Jews, and the emphasis throughout the prayer is on God's people. In 9:7, M speaks of the confusion which has been brought לאיש יהודה וליושבי ירושלם ולכל ישראל which equals the OG ανθρωποις ιουδα και καθημενοις εν ιερουσαλημ και παντι τω λαω ισραηλ "to the people of Judah and those dwelling in Jerusalem and to all the people of Israel." The OG faithfully translates these references, and inserts τω λαω *ad sensum*. The emphasis in the prayer throughout is upon כל ישראל = πας ισραηλ "all of Israel" (9:11). When Daniel entreats God to forgive the sinful people, again the references are to Israel and to Jerusalem. Moreover, the references in 9:16 are faithfully translated: ירושלם הר קדשך = ιερουσαλημ ορους του αγιου σου "Jerusalem, thy holy mountain"; אבותינו = των πατερων ημων "our ancestors"; ירושלם = ιερουσαλημ; עמך = δημος σου "your people." There is no attempt to include anyone other than Jews where "the people" are concerned. If we examine two further references where the OG would have had an opportunity to include foreign groups we find further indication of the fidelity to the meaning of the *Vorlage*. In 7:27 we read that the kingdom יהיבת לעם קדישי עליונין = εδωκε λαω αγιω υψιστου "shall be given to the people of the saints of the Most High" OG, and in 12:1, at the time of the end, Michael is referred to as העמד על בני עמך = ο εστηκως επι τους υιους του λαου σου "the one who stands for the sons of your people." And in the reference in 12:1b, עמך כל הנמצא כתוב בספר = πας ο λαος ος αν ευρεθη εγγεγραμμενος εν τω βιβλιω "your people, everyone

found written in the book," with the variant πας ο λαος for כל עמך due to the
final *kap* of עמך having been omitted because of the following *kap* of כל.
The OG reads עם כל instead of the correct עמך כל, thus yielding πας ο λαος.

We may conclude that the OG does not necessarily give us any consistent indication of greater universalism as Bruce implies. Certainly there is no consistent pattern. Although Bruce's position is possible, it is not the best way to understand this reading. We believe that our reading is more in line with what we have observed about the faithful nature of the OG translator elsewhere. Our investigation of the OG word choice for עם as well as the context of Daniel 9 and two other references to the people of Israel in 7:27 and 12:1 shows that the understanding of the OG does not alter the thought expressed in Daniel M.

The Political Attitude toward
the Ptolemies and Seleucids

Chapter 11 of Daniel presents a detailed, elaborate view of history in which the Persians, Alexander the Great, and significant kings of the Seleucid and Ptolemaic line play an important role. This history would have been of great interest to the OG translator, as it was for the author of Daniel, since the events, some of which had already taken place, and others which were predicted, were close to the translator's time and interest. In our examination of the OG of Daniel 11, is it possible to find any examples of *Tendenz* wherein the translator's attitude toward the political groups or events may be discerned? We are especially interested in the OG translator's attitude toward the Ptolemies and Seleucids since it existed in an era where their struggles were in the forefront of events and interest.

Although the majority of historical references in Daniel consist of the struggles between the Ptolemies and Seleucids, the struggles between the Persians and Greeks also play an important role. We wish to investigate the OG in order to see whether the translator showed any particular prejudice in treating one group as opposed to the other, or perhaps the translation gives us references which are germane to the translator's own time or interest. References to Persia in Daniel 7–12 are found in 7:6; 8:3–4,6–7,20; 10:1, 13,20; 11:1 (ο′ θ′) and 11:2. We turn to examine the noteworthy variants which could possibly be an indication of *Tendenz*.

The first example concerns one of the characteristics of the leopard which, in Daniel's first vision, represents Persia. Does the translator reveal an attitude toward the Persians which is not present in the Aramaic text?

7:6

M 4QDanᵃ   ושלטן יהיב לה

o' 967   και γλωσσα εδοθη αυτω

θ'   και εξουσια εδοθη αυτη

OG errs, reading לשן "tongue" for שלטן "dominion," metathesis of *šin* and *lāmed* and omission of *ṭēt*.[22] Yet McCrystall sees the reading of γλωσσα "tongue" as an example of intentional change on the part of the translator who included this so that "the Persian kingdom is portrayed as having a human quality (γλωσσα) just as did the the Babylonian (vii 4 ανθρωπινη καρδια): but no such quality is attributed to the kingdom of Greece."[23] This verse is used as part of McCrystall's data to argue that the OG portrays the Persians in a positive light since they were enemies of the Seleucids just as the Ptolemies were (here the Seleucids are equated with the Greeks). And since the OG translator was pro-Ptolemaic, so too was the translator pro-Persian in McCrystall's argument.

In this particular example, we would argue, if the OG did indeed alter the meaning of the text by using a positive description for the leopard when there was no basis in the *Vorlage,* then McCrystall might be able to use this example as relevant data for an indication of the OG's attitude toward Persia. We have two objections, however. First of all, the sense of the Greek itself does not warrant such far-reaching claims. Obviously, γλωσσα is a characteristic of an animal as well as a human. It is not necessarily an indication of speech. Both M and o' use a different word for the horn which spoke, namely פם = στομα "mouth" found in 7:8. Secondly, we have seen the frequency with which the OG errs. A simple metathesis accounts for this error. γλωσσα probably made sense to the translator since the verse deals with the characteristics of the body of this beast.

The next significant variants concerning Persia are found in 11:1–2.

11:1

4QDanᶜ   [בשנת אחת לדריוש המדי עמדתי למחזק
              ולמעוז לו

M   ואני בשנת אחת לדריוש המדי עמדי למחזיק
              ולמעוז לו

o'   και εν τω ενιαυτω τω πρωτω κυρου του βασιλεως ειπε μοι
             ενισχυσαι και ανδριζεσθαι

θ'   και εγω εν ετει πρωτω κυρου εστην εις κρατος και ισχυν

McCrystall argues that the OG translator uses εν τω ενιαυτω τω πρωτω κυρου του βασιλεως "in the first year of Cyrus the King" instead of the M reading

[22] Montgomery, *A Critical and Exegetical Commentary,* 295.
[23] McCrystall, "Studies in the Old Greek Translation of Daniel," 301.

בשנת אחת לדריוש המדי "in the first year of Darius the Mede" in order to allow for consistency with 10:1.[24] In 10:1, M refers to the third year of Cyrus, בשנת שלוש, whereas the o′ text has the first year of Cyrus εν τω ενιαυτω τω πρωτω. We have already shown that the third year of Cyrus was in the original OG, and that the o′ text which has πρωτω is not the original but rather a later copyist's error for τριτω. But having accepted the o′ text as the OG, McCrystall argues that the OG used "in the first year of Cyrus" intentionally in both 10:1 and 11:1 so that the context of chapter 10 is preeminent in the reader's mind until the end of chapter 11. Besides saying that the OG translation of 10:1 and 11:1 make for one unit, McCrystall adds no further elaboration. We do agree that chapters 10 and 11 are indeed one unit for all versions of Daniel (M, o′, θ′) since the later rabbinical and medieval chapter divisions, by separating 10:22 from 11:1, disrupt Gabriel's speech. The separation was inserted here, no doubt, because of the reference to the time frame.[25] We note that Gabriel uses the time reference simply to say that Michael has been with him a length of time; it is not a reference to a new vision.

In our own investigation of 11:1 we find that the OG does not change what is present in the *Vorlage* to conform with the date found in 10:1, *pace* McCrystall. We find that the *Vorlage* was different from the text now preserved in M. The following words require comment. The OG reads ειπε = ענה "he answered" for ואני "and I." θ′ χαι εγω = M "and I." The OG reads לי = μοι "to me" for לו "to him," and θ′ ignores לו. For לדריוש "of Darius" both o′ and θ′ have χυρου "Cyrus." This can best be explained if כרוש "Cyrus" were in the *Vorlage* since θ′ would be especially careful to translate this accurately. Here we disagree with Montgomery who maintains that Darius is prior and argues, "this change in name by assimilation with 10:1, [is] correct historically, but [is] counter to the view of the b[oo]k that the Medes overthrew that empire."[26] We suggest that the Greek readings are not only prior, but that the pattern of historiography for the author of the book of Daniel was indeed Babylon (7:1, 8:1), Media (9:1), and Persia (10:1). Moreover, in the context of chapters 10 and 11, which is one unit consisting of Gabriel's speech, Gabriel's time reference is indeed to Cyrus. It seems unlikely that Darius should be introduced. We suggest that the original Hebrew text had כרוש "Cyrus," and a later Hebrew copyist's error confused *kap* and *dālet* and wrote דרוש or דריוש "Darius." This must have occurred before α′ and σ′, since they have δαρειου του μηδου "Darius the Mede" according to Syh. Thus, דריוש is reflected in 4QDanᶜ. The OG does add an editorial expansion by inserting του βασιλεως "the king," an addition for

---

Ibid., 271–72.
[25] Montgomery, *A Critical and Exegetical Commentary*, 417.
[26] Ibid., 418–19.

clarification.[27] המדי "the Mede" is a later addition to the original Hebrew, most likely a gloss on the error דריוש, or a corrupted dittography for עמדי "I stood." Once the error דריוש was made for כרוש, the word עמדי was mistakenly read as המדי (similar sounds and letters). Concerning עמדי, note that 4QDan^c reads עמדתי, substituting the *qal* perfect for the infinitive absolute. This tradition gives further evidence that the form of עמדי was difficult in this context and may have contributed to the OG variant reading. Note also the use of *final mēm* in למחזק and ולמעוז.

Our investigation of these variants in 11:1 shows that the OG accurately translated a Hebrew *Vorlage* which then underwent change at a stage later than the OG. Therefore, claims may not be imposed upon the OG of 11:1 to argue that an intentional historical change at the level of translation has occurred.

Continuing with the OG translator's historiography McCrystall argues that the putative change of the M reading, Darius the Mede, to the OG reading, Cyrus the King in 11:1 also leads to another historical change in 11:2. The first phrase McCrystall considers reads:

11:2

M 4QDan^c	הנה עוד שלשה מלכים עמדים לפרס
o′	ιδου τρεις βασιλεις ανθεστηκασιν εν τη περσιδι
θ′	ιδου ετι τρεις βασιλεις αναστησονται εν τη περσιδι

McCrystall argues that the M reading עמדים "shall arise" is translated with the OG ανθεστηκασιν "opposed" because the use of the perfect is appropriate to the OG who believes mistakenly that the Persians Xerxes and Darius precede Cyrus and that all these kings are part of the *Persian* resistance to the Greek empire.[28] McCrystall maintains that since the OG translator believes that Xerxes and Darius are Persian and precede Cyrus, the translator thus uses the past perfect ανθεστηκασιν to refer to the kings who have already resisted. We would argue, however, that the OG translator either mistakenly read the finite form of the verb for the participle, or was not careful about the tense equivalences, as often occurs elsewhere. We do not believe that the translator was identifying these kings implicitly in 11:2, against McCrystall who holds that for the OG, the three kings are indeed identified with the past Persian rulers, Xerxes, Darius, and Cyrus. Rather, we hold that the OG follows the same pattern of historiography that parallels M: Babylonians, Medians, Persians, Greeks. Both the Hebrew texts and the

---

[27] An alternative suggestion would be that מלך was in the *Vorlage,* and according to Kennicott and de Rossi, a manuscript does indeed preserve מלך, although this could be an independent error.

[28] McCrystall, "Studies in the Old Greek Translation of Daniel," 299–300.

OG have used a fictitious Darius to refer to a king of Media who preceded Cyrus the Persian, instead of the historically accurate Darius II the Persian who follows Cyrus, Ahasuerus (Xerxes), and Artaxerxes I. Neither the OG nor M have unequivocal references to the three Persian kings of 11:2. But for all versions of Daniel, the three kings are important primarily because they climax in a fourth who must fight with Alexander. There is no evidence that the OG changed this, as the Greek translator does not alter this sequence or reference, and McCrystall goes beyond the meaning of the OG based upon the OG's use of a less literal verb tense.

Our final reading in 11:2 which merits consideration concerns the fighting activity of the fourth king of Persia against the kingdom of Greece. The phrase in question reads:

M	מלכות יון
o′	βασιλει ελληνων
θ′	βασιλειαις ελληνων

McCrystall argues that the OG choice "enables him to bring out the continuous opposition of the Persians to successive Greek kings," and that the OG thus "shows an interest in the continuous harassment of the Greek kings by Persia."[29] In response, first of all we would note that whether the Persians fight the Greek kingdom (βασιλεια) or the Greek King (βασιλευς), the meaning is the same. Secondly, as shown in Chapter III, it would not be unusual for the translator to use βασιλευς for מלכות as a stylistic change, since the translator is not always concerned with exact equivalencies.

To conclude this section on the OG translator's attitude toward the Persians, we note that in our investigation of the references to Persia found in Daniel 8 (8:3–4, 6–7) in our Chapter II above, that except for minor stylistic changes, the descriptions of the beasts representing Persia remain intact. The OG does not alter the animal description.

In Daniel 8, the OG shows no lessening of the destructive power of Persia on the part of the OG translator. We may conclude that the references to Persia may not be used as evidence to support McCrystall's theory that only the OG ameliorates the references to Persia since they preview the struggle of the Ptolemies, which the OG supposedly favors, over the Seleucids.

We turn now to some of the key verses upon which McCrystall builds his argument for the supposed pro-Ptolemaic attitude of the OG translator. We have previously examined Dan 11:25 in Chapter IV. We now turn to Dan 11:7 and 11:10.

---

[29] Ibid., 302.

11:7

M	ועשה בהם והחזיק
ο′	και ποιησει ταραχην και κατισχυσει
θ′	και ποιησει εν αυτοις και κατισχυσει

The OG reading ταραχην "tumult" does not equal the M reading בהם "in them." McCrystall argues that the OG translator chooses ταραχη to underscore Ptolemy's activity as God's instrument. We note, first of all, that the *author* of Daniel interprets history theologically, and thus ultimately every activity of the empire is subordinate to the Lord's plans. Moreover, as Montgomery suggests, the OG use of ταραχην could be accounted for by the OG reading of מהומה "tumult" for בהם as is done in Isa 22:5. ταραχην is never used elsewhere in Daniel ο′ θ′; thus it is difficult to conclude that its employment here is evidence of a new slant.

11:10

M	יתגרו ואספו
ο′	και ερεθισθησεται και συναξει
θ′	συναξουσιν

McCrystall focuses upon the OG translation of יתגרו "will wage war" used twice in 11:10. He argues that in the first instance, ερεθιζειν "rouse to fight, provoke" has an "evil connotation" and was deliberately chosen because the translator goes beyond the text in order to deprecate the Seleucids as much as possible. We note, in contrast, that ερεθιζειν is not restricted to the Seleucids alone, but is rather found for the Ptolemies as well in 11:25, again used to translate יתגרה. We examined this reading above, in Chapter IV.

In our assessment of Daniel 11, we would agree with McCrystall that the OG may employ paraphrases, use a wider vocabulary than θ′ in the translation, and contains translation which differs from the sense of M because of mechanical error. However, as the above examples show, we do not find it necessary to impute theological *Tendenz* to account for the motivation of the translator. Rather, these examples, which are akin to what we saw in Chapter II above, typify the translation of the OG.

The Time of the End

In turning to Dan 9:24–27 we face a difficult challenge of the OG text, since there are a great number of variants in the ο′ text. As a background for the understanding of the OG translation of the interpretation of the prophecy of the seventy weeks, we pause to examine 7:25; 8:14; 9:2; 12:7; 12:11;

and 12:13, since all of these verses give predictions concerning the time of the end.

7:25

M   עד עדן ועדנין ופלג עדן

o′   εως καιρου και καιρων και εως ημισους καιρου

θ′   εως καιρου και καιρων και ημισυ καιρου

o′ adds the second εως, but it is clear that the meaning of M is preserved in o′ "for a time and two times and for half a time." θ′ = M "for a time and two times and half a time."

8:14

M   עד ערב בקר אלפים ושלש מאות

o′   εως εσπερας και πρωι ημεραι δισχιλιαι τριακοσιαι

θ′   εως εσπερας και πρωι ημεραι δισχιλιαι και τριακοσιαι

o′ and θ′ accurately translate M, although the presence of ημεραι "days" in both Greek texts may reflect a *Vorlage* which had יומים. But whether we read with the Greek texts, "for 2300 evenings and mornings are the days," or with M, "for 2300 evenings and mornings," the meaning is the same.

9:2

M   שבעים שנה

o′ θ′   εβδομηκοντα ετη

M = o′ = θ′ "seventy years."

12:7

M   למועד מועדים וחצי

o′   εις καιρον και καιρους και ημισυ καιρου

θ′   εις καιρον καιρων και ημισυ καιρου

M = θ′ "for a time, two times and half a time." o′ adds και "for a time and two times and half a time."

12:11

M   ימים אלף מאתים ותשעים

o′   ημερας χιλιας διακοσιας ενενηκοντα

θ′   ημεραι χιλιαι διακοσιαι ενενηκοντα

o′ and θ′ both accurately translate M "a thousand two hundred and ninety days."

12:12

M   לימים אלף שלש מאות שלשים וחמשה

ο' θ'   εις ημερας χιλιας τριαχοσιας τριαχοντα πεντε

All three texts are equal (to the thousand three hundred and thirty-five days). We note that in all these time references, the OG is faithful to the meaning of the Semitic *Vorlage*.

Is the OG translator similarly faithful to the text in 9:24–27 or does the translator provide us with a unique rendering which may be indicative of a unique theological perspective? In attempting to answer this question we must keep in mind that we cannot be certain of the original Hebrew text. α' and σ' presuppose a variant text and in some cases the θ' and ο' texts do so as well. We may assume that it is the content of these verses which led to the reworked nature of the text. Just as 9:24–27 is an interpretation of the seventy weeks in Jeremiah's prophecy, so too have later scribes attempted to interpret its explanation. It must be acknowledged that one must proceed cautiously in understanding the variants to be of great theological weight. Bludau was one of the first scholars to provide a comprehensive examination of the variants of the OG, and he contends that important theological statements are being made which reflect the later date of the OG translator who would have lived during Judas Maccabeus's triumph.[30] Although Montgomery does not propose a comprehensive theological interpretation of the OG, he does believe that the variant in v 27 concerning the removal of the desolation refers to Judas Maccabeus's success.[31] Moreover, Bruce remarks that the variant in 9:26 points to an "astonishing interpretation" on the part of the Greek translator.

We turn now to particular variants in 9:24–27. The most striking variant in 9:24 reads

M   ולמשח קדש קדשים

ο'   χαι ευφραναι αγιον αγιων

θ'   χαι του χρισαι αγιον αγιων

M = θ' "and to anoint a most holy place/thing/one," yet the OG reads differently "and to rejoice [in?] a most holy place/thing/one." It is clear that the OG misread ולשמח "and to rejoice" for ולמשח, "and to anoint" which he translated with ευφραναι.[32] Even though Bludau acknowledges that ευφραναι can be accounted for with the metathesis, he claims that the verb ευφραναι which refers to the rejoicing over the fulfillment of Jeremiah's

[30] Bludau, "Die alexandrinische Uebersetzung des Buches Daniel," 126.

[31] Montgomery, *A Critical and Exegetical Commentary*, 395.

[32] Ibid., 377.

prophecy, makes sense only if it refers to a person, and not to a thing or place. Thus, he argues, αγιον αγιων refers to Daniel himself or to the high priest who is to lead the Jews out of imprisonment.[33] Yet two objections may be made here. First, the following verse (9:25) makes it clear that it is indeed the temple to which the author and translator are referring, for here we read of the rebuilding of Jerusalem. Secondly, we find in 9:26 o′ that the city (την πολιν) and sanctuary (το αγιον) are to be destroyed. Clearly we should not discount the context and posit theological motivation when a simple metathesis can account for the variant. Moreover, the reading לשמח is again witnessed to in a doublet translation in the beginning of 9:25. The texts read:

M	ותדע ותשכל
o′	και γνωση και διανοηθηση και ευφρανθηση
θ′	και γνωση και συνησεις

M = θ′ "and you will know and understand." The o′ plus, ευφρανθηση "you shall rejoice," is from לשמח.

A second variant in 9:25 that is brought to our attention by Bludau is the following:

M	ולבנות ירושלם עד משיח נגיד
o′	και οικοδομησεις ιερουσαλημ πολιν κυριω
θ′	και του οικοδομησαι ιερουσαλημ εως χριστου ηγουμενου

It is clear that the OG translator misread עיר "city" for עד "until"; the similarities of *reš* and *dālet* prompt this confusion, and the absence of the internal *mater lectionis* can be accounted for by defective spelling. Moreover, after seeing ירושלם "Jerusalem" the translator could understandably expect to see עיר. The reading κυριω "Lord" for משיח נגיד "an anointed one, a prince" stands as a singular translation. We cannot be certain whether it was actually in the OG, or whether it occurred at a later stage. We should note that commentators have found this translation problematic. Montgomery holds that the translator omits משיח and is translating נגיד when employing κυριω.[34] Yet, in the o′ text of Daniel, κυριος is used to translate אדני (9:3,4,7; 10:19), יהוה (9:4,10,13,14,20), אלוהים (9:15; 10:12) and neither in the Greek texts of Daniel nor in other Greek translations of the Hebrew Bible do we find κυριος used to translate נגיד or משיח. Bludau is correct in seeing this as an interpretation on the part of the translator, yet he assigns a speculative interpretation when he contends that this was employed because the OG translator understood the משיח נגיד to be God himself, or at least the person

---

who would be both high priest (which he understands is meant by מֹשִׁיח) and worldly ruler (נָגִיד).[35] Yet even though later texts understood this reference to be messianic, as the Syriac has "unto King Messiah" and the Vulgate reads "ad Christum ducem,"[36] it is clear that this reference is simply speaking of the city Jerusalem, which the OG translator designates as the city of the Lord. In 9:16 (o'), in Daniel's prayer to God, Daniel asks God to turn his anger απο της πολεως σου ιερουσαλημ "away from your city, Jerusalem" (= M). In 9:18, Daniel asks God to behold της πολεως σου εφ ης επεκληθη το ονομα σου επ αυτης "your city which is called by your name." Clearly, the connection of Jerusalem as the city of God was obvious.

A third variant in 9:25 which calls for comment is the rendering of לבנות = οικοδομησαι θ' "to build," as οικοδομησεις "*you* will build" in the OG. Bludau holds that by using οικοδομησεις the translator believed that God was addressing Daniel in the prophecy.[37] For this translator, he maintains, the message of the rebuilding of Jerusalem is identical with the word spoken to Daniel. Therefore, Daniel himself would rebuild the city or at least encourage its reconstruction by his influence at the Persian court. We may, however, more plausibly suggest that the OG translator rendered לבנות as the second person singular οικοδομησεις, addressed to Daniel, because of the preceding series of verbs γνωση και διανοθηση και ευφρανθηση και ευρησεις "know and understand and you will rejoice and you will find" which are also addressed to Daniel.

Of special interest is 9:26 because of a variant in the number of weeks that will occur before the anointing will be cut off (αποσταθησεται χρισμα). Is this an attempt at interpretation on the part of the OG translator? Bruce states that "perhaps the earliest attempt to interpret the seventy heptads may be recognized in the paraphrase of Dn ix 24–27 in the older Greek version of the book. . . . At the beginning of verse 26 there is an astonishing alteration of the original text."[38] The o' text has 77 and 62 instead of simply 62 years, as do the texts of M and θ'. Bruce argues that the translator presents a total of 139 years which corresponds to the time reference in 1 Macc 1:10 where the 137th year of the kingdom of the Greeks refers to the beginning of the reign of Antiochus.[39] Thus, the Greek translator understood that the removal of the anointed one (Onias III) occurred two years after Antiochus came to power, or in 139 (= 137 + 2). We must note, however, that it is not

[35] Bludau, "Die alexandrinische Uebersetzung des Buches Daniel," 120.
[36] Montgomery, *A Critical and Exegetical Commentary*, 378.
[37] Bludau, "Die alexandrinische Uebersetzung des Buches Daniel," 120.
[38] F. F. Bruce, "The Earliest Old Testament Interpretation," 44.
[39] Ibid.

certain in which year Onias was removed from power[40] and there is no evidence from the o' text that the OG translator was privy to any additional information.

The texts of 9:26 read:

M	ואחרי השבעים ששים ושנים
o'	και μετα επτα και εβδομηκοντα και εξηκοντα δυο
θ'	και μετα τας εβδομαδας τας εξηκοντα δυο
α'	και μετα τας επτα και εβδομαδας δυο
σ'	και μετα τας εβδομαδας τας επτα και εξηκοντα δυο

We now proceed to examine different possibilities to account for the variation in o'.

Possibility A. If we presume that the *Vorlage* of the OG = M, then it is possible that the OG misread הַשִּׁבְעִים for הַשָּׁבֻעִים and thus used εβδομηκοντα "seventy" instead of the correct εβδομαδας "weeks." We would understand that the next stage was the later insertion of επτα και "and seven."

Possibility B. Perhaps the OG had a different *Vorlage,* or misread it as follows: ואחרי שבעה וששים ושנים = και μετα επτα και εξηκοντα δυο "and after seven and sixty-two." Later the mistake was corrected by the insertion of εβδομηκοντα "weeks," but επτα was not removed. Thus, the OG: και μετα επτα και εβδομηκοντα και εξηκοντα δυο.

After noting both possibilities we must remember the context in which 9:26 is found. We would argue that επτα is not an error, but a clarification. Thus, we find possibility A more plausible since it shows that επτα was indeed an insertion, which was added by the OG translator to clarify the time sequence of the prophecy of the seventy weeks. According to the Masoretic text of 9:24–27 the seventy weeks of Jeremiah's prophecy are divided into three periods. First, from the issuance of the word concerning the rebuilding of Jerusalem to the coming of the anointed one there are seven weeks (9:25). Secondly, the anointed one will be cut off after 62 weeks (9:26). Thirdly, one week will be characterized by the covenant made with many by the "prince who is to come" (7 + 62 + 1). In 9:26 of the OG, the translator has inserted επτα to clarify the fact that the anointed one (who will be cut off after 62 weeks, if the terminus a quo is the rebuilding of Jerusalem) will be cut off after 62 + 7 years with the terminus a quo being the issuance of the word. We have already shown that εβδομηκοντα comes from a misreading of שבעים. To add 70 + 7 + 62 and reckon the total as being understood to have its terminus

---

[40] See the chronology of Elias Bickerman, *The God of the Maccabees* (Leiden: Brill), 1979.

a quo from the issuance of the word, as Bruce does, is to assign a significance to the OG translation that the OG translator would not have recognized.

One might object that the OG does not preserve the same three-fold division of the seventy weeks since 9:25 (o') does not specify that the rebuilding of Jerusalem will take place after seven weeks and that 9:25 o' does not include the reference that "then for sixty-two weeks it shall be built again with squares and moat but in a troubled time." However, it must be remembered that the o' text is only an inexact witness to the OG. The omission may be accounted for by the frequency of the use of שׁבעים "weeks" in 9:25–26 and the repetition of ושׁבעים שׁשׁים שׁנים in 9:25–26. We may note that the reading of 9:25 ושׁבעים שׁשׁים ושׁנים תשׁוב ונבנתה רחוב וחרוץ ובצוק העתים "and for sixty-two weeks it shall be built again, street and moat but in distress of the times" is found not in 9:25 of the o' text, but part of it has been misplaced in 9:27 και παλιν επιϲρεφει και ανοικοδομηθηϲεται εις πλατος και μηκος και κατα ϲυντελειαν καιρων "and again it will return and be built up in breadth and length but at the end of times." Compare the reading in 9:27: και μετα επτα και εβδομηκοντα καιρους και εξηκοντα δυο ετη "and after seven and seventy times and sixty-two years." We must note that καιρους and ετη are two more examples of explanatory additions and are not further examples of interpretative activity at the level of the translator as Bruce suggests.

A final possible objection to the threefold time schema in 9:27 is that in the OG the covenant is to be made επι πολλας εβδομαδας "for many weeks" instead of שׁבוע אחד (= εβδομας μια "for one week," θ', α'). However, it is possible that επι πολλας is a doublet translation for לרבים "for many."

The last problem which needs to be addressed concerning 9:24–27 is the final picture or world outlook that is present in the OG text. Both Bludau and Montgomery find that a more optimistic view is presented on the part of the OG translator. Montgomery points to 9:27 which reads in part: [. . . και αφαιρεθηϲεται η ερημωϲις] εν τω κατιϲχυϲαι την διαθηκην επι πολλας εβδομαδας "and the desolation will be removed in the enforcing of the covenant for many weeks" which "doubtless refers to Judas' triumph."[41] Bludau holds that the prophecy concludes with a view full of hope because the translator has experienced the success of the Maccabees.[42] In fact, he sees the discussion concerning the rebuilding of the temple in 9:27 to refer to the rebuilding of the city by the Maccabees, who had to reconstruct Jerusalem after the damage that Antiochus inflicted upon the city especially that done by Apollonius. To respond to Montgomery, we must note that although the reading to which he refers in 9:27 is indeed a variant, it can be seen that it

---

[41] Montgomery, *A Critical and Exegetical Commentary,* 395.
[42] Bludau, "Die alexandrinische Uebersetzung des Buches Daniel," 127-28.

is a corrupt doublet translation for נחרצת שממות והגביר ברית לרבים
"desolations are decreed and he will make a covenant with many" (9:26–27).
Moreover, this variant could have been introduced into the text at a time
later than the OG translation, and we note that Ziegler suggests that και
αφαιρεθησεται η ερημωσις is indeed secondary. Responding to Bludau, we note
that the reference to the rebuilding of Jerusalem in 9:27 is a displacement
from 9:25 where it would have originally stood in the OG. There is no
evidence that the translator is making specific claims that it is the Maccabees
who are doing the rebuilding.

Our conclusions concerning 9:24–27 do not deny that there are pluses,
minuses, and variants in the OG text. Since it is clear, however, that the
variants can be accounted for by plausible misreading of the Hebrew text and
by later shifting of phrases, we need not impute theological motivation to
explain the variants of the OG translation. Moreover, the witness of α′ σ′ and
others attest to the fact that the present Masoretic text itself has undergone
revision and differs from the *Vorlage* upon which the OG version was based.
It is true that later Jewish and Christian interpreters relied on variant Greek
translations, errors, and glosses to support their own theological claims, but
at the level of translation the OG translator thought that the sense of the
Vorlage was being accurately preserved.

This chapter has investigated five readings of particular interest in the
study of the OG of Daniel. Past studies have claimed that the OG variants
in the above cited readings are evidence of the particular thematic, theological or historical perspectives of the OG translator which go beyond the
intention of the original text. We have argued, however, that these texts
should not be viewed in isolation, but rather that passages which deal with
the same theme should be investigated equally. In all these cases of putative
Tendenz we have seen that a contextual examination supports the theory that
these variants are errors. The OG translator was attempting to present an
accurate translation and did not use these occasions to insert personal ideas
which would be indicative of a distinct perspective.

VI

CONCLUSION

In order to assess the character of the OG of Daniel 7–12 and to investigate the possibility of theological *Tendenz* on the part of the translator this study has proceeded through five stages.

First of all, our investigation of the manuscript evidence and of the history and stratigraphy of the texts of Daniel showed that the Semitic text of Daniel has undergone growth and change and that the *Vorlage* available to the OG translator was not necessarily equal to the present day Masoretic text. Therefore, simply to note where the OG diverges from M and then posit reasons for that divergence, as past studies have done, is too simplistic an approach to use as a basis for assessing "theological *Tendenz* on the part of the OG translator." The possibility that the OG is faithful to its own divergent *Vorlage* must also be considered and indeed accounts for some of the variants in the OG of Daniel. Both our reconstruction of the OG and evidence from the extant Qumran fragments verified this understanding. We also noted that the texts labeled o′ and θ′ may sometimes be other than the true OG and the true Theodotionic recension. The OG text may actually be found in 967 or even in the θ′ text because of Origen's errors in compiling the Hexapla. Critical use of 967, Ziegler's reconstructed texts in the Göttingen edition, and our knowledge of recensional theory and OG characteristics help prevent such unnuanced equations.

Secondly, we have shown that before an assessment can be made concerning OG readings which seem to diverge from the Semitic text we must first be familiar with the typical character of the OG when it is accurately translating the Semitic *Vorlage*. We have shown in our sample continuous passage that the OG tries to render faithfully the *Vorlage* into well-constructed Greek prose. However, unlike the recension of θ′, the OG is not concerned with standardizing roots or grammatical forms and employs a much wider vocabulary. For these reasons, it is fair to say that the OG is a freer translation than that of θ′. However, we noted in our sample test cases, as well as in the sample continuous passage, that the OG is reasonably accurate and faithful. The evidence from this part of our investigation provides an important cautionary note for assessing possible *Tendenz* when the OG employs an unusual word in translating one particular Semitic root. We have shown that employing a diverse vocabulary and being unconcerned with standardization of roots or of grammatical forms is simply a typical characteristic of the translation as a whole.

Thirdly, our section on the mechanical variants in the OG showed that the translator did indeed err when reading the words and deciphering the letters of words in the *Vorlage*. We listed many examples of these cases wherein an examination of the meaning of the OG in comparison to the meaning of the Semitic text showed that nothing of interpretative value was at stake. This demonstrated that it cannot be assumed that all instances of change of meaning in the OG text are prompted by a particular agenda on the part of the OG translator. Rather, errors occurred throughout the text, most of which were due to the unintentional cross-linguistic mechanics of translation.

Fourthly, this study has demonstrated that some variant readings now embedded in the o′ text come from post-OG emendations, corruptions, or additions to the original OG translation. Thus, certain claims made by modern interpreters of the OG needed to be reevaluated; we showed that putative interpretative activity on the part of the OG translator concerning the Ancient of Days, the dating of Cyrus's tenure, the attitude toward the Ptolemies, and those who rise from the dust of the earth were based upon readings in the o′ text that post-dated the true OG.

Fifthly, in examining true OG variants whose meaning hinted at possible theological *Tendenz* in the broader context of other Dan OG passages which contain the same or similar word, idea, or meaning, we have argued that the OG translator was not attempting to depart from the meaning or implications of the Semitic *Vorlage* in selected passages wherein that claim had been made. Rather, our more complete investigation of these references showed that the OG translator faithfully translated them in all other instances in the text. This evidence, along with the fact that the single attestations of each of the variants can be accounted for by the same types of mechanical errors that the OG translator makes in the translation where no hint of intentionality can be imputed, led us to conclude confidently that the translator is not engaging in any particular interpretative activity.

Thus, our over-all assessment maintains that the OG translator of Daniel 7–12 attempted to translate accurately the *Vorlage* available of the day. In the attempt to translate, the OG translator was most concerned with conveying an accurate rendering in Greek of the Semitic text available. If, on occasion, this required that an antecedent be expressed, a phrase in apposition be added, a paraphrase be used, or that one particular connotation of a word be emphasized, the translator felt free to do so. However, these changes were not made to depart intentionally from the meaning of the Semitic text. The OG translator was more concerned with providing an interesting and readable Greek style than a consistent, standardized translation. A variety of syntactical and grammatical usages, a wide vocabulary, and picturesque speech characterize the work. These features are especially noticeable when the OG is compared with the recension of θ′. It is true that the OG translator of Daniel was apt to err. These mechanical errors are understandable, however, when we consider the paleography of the day. It is precisely this tendency which has led commentators to judge the OG translator to be engaging in theological *Tendenz*. However, we have shown that the supposed tendentious readings must be investigated text-critically to see whether the divergence from the meaning of M may be accounted for by mechanical error or by secondary emendations. We have demonstrated that the OG translator did not undertake the work with a particular agenda. Although contemporary Jewish writers were writing commentaries on their sacred texts, the translator of Daniel 7–12 did not hold that translation was the proper forum for the theological interpretation of the readings of the sacred text.

SELECT BIBLIOGRAPHY

Albright, W. F. "New Light on Early Recensions of the Hebrew Bible."
BASOR 140 (1955) 27–33.

Barr, J. *Comparative Philology and the Text of the Old Testament*. Oxford:
Clarendon, 1968.

Barthélemy, D. *Les Devanciers d'Aquila*. VTSup 10. Leiden: Brill, 1963.

———. *Études d'histoire du texte de l'Ancien Testament*. OBO 21. Fribourg:
Éditions universitaires, and Göttingen: Vandenhoeck and Ruprecht,
1978.

Bevan, A. A. *A Short Commentary on the Book of Daniel*. Cambridge:
University, 1892.

Biblia Hebraica. Ed. R. Kittel et al. 12th ed. Stuttgart: Privilegierte württembergische Bibelanstalt, 1961.

Biblia Hebraica Stuttgartensia. Ed. K. Elliger and W. Rudolph. Stuttgart:
Deutsche Bibelstiftung, 1977.

Bickerman, E. "Some Notes on the Transmission of the Septuagint," *A.
Marx Jubilee Volume*. New York: n. p., 1950.

Birnbaum, S. A. *Hebrew Scripts*. Leiden: Brill, 1971.

Bludau, A. "Die alexandrinische Uebersetzung des Buches Daniel und ihr
Verhältniss zum massorethischen Text," *BibS*(F) II, 2–3 (1897) v–218.

Bodine, W. *The Greek Text of Judges: Recensional Developments*. HSM 23.
Chico: Scholars, 1980.

Brock, S. P., Fritsch, C. T., and Jellicoe, S. *A Classified Bibliography of
the Septuagint*. Leiden: Brill, 1973.

Brown, F., Driver, S. R., and Briggs, C. A. *A Hebrew and English Lexicon
of the Old Testament*. Oxford: Clarendon, 1952.

Bruce, F. F. "The Earliest Old Testament Interpretation." *OTS* 17 (1972)
37–52.

———. "Prophetic Interpretation in the Septuagint." *BIOSCS* 12 (1979)
17–26.

———. "The Oldest Greek Version of Daniel," *OTS* 20 (1975) 22–40.

Charles, R. H. *The Book of Daniel*. Oxford: Oxford University, 1913.

———. *A Critical and Exegetical Commentary on the Book of Daniel.* Oxford: Clarendon, 1929.

Cross, F. M. *The Ancient Library of Qumran and Modern Biblical Studies.* Rev. ed. Garden City: Anchor, 1961.

———. "The Development of the Jewish Scripts." *The Bible and the Ancient Near East: Essays in Honor of William Foxwell Albright,* 170–264. Ed. G. E. Wright. Garden City: Doubleday, 1961.

———. "Editing the Manuscript Fragments from Qumran: Cave 4 of Qumran (4Q)." *BA* 19 (1956) 86.

———. "The Evolution of a Theory of Local Texts." *Qumran and the History of the Biblical Text,* 306–20. Ed. F. M. Cross and S. Talmon. Cambridge: Harvard University, 1975.

———. "The History of the Biblical Text in the Light of Discoveries in the Judaean Desert," *HTR* 57 (1964) 281–99.

Deist, F. E. *Toward the Text of the Old Testament.* Pretoria: D. R. Church Booksellers, 1978.

Field, F. *Hexaplarum quae supersunt.* Oxford: Clarendon, 1875.

Fitzmyer, J. A. *The Dead Sea Scrolls: Major Publications and Tools for Study.* SBLSBS 8; Missoula: Scholars, 1977.

Geissen, A. *Der Septuaginta-Text des Buches Daniel nach dem Kölner Teil des Papyrus 967: Kap. V–XII.* Bonn: R. Habelt, 1968.

Gesenius, W., Kautzsch, E., and Cowley, A. E. *Hebrew Grammar.* 2nd ed. Oxford: Clarendon, 1910.

Ginsberg, H. L. *Studies in Daniel.* New York: Jewish Theological Seminary of America, 1948.

Gooding, D. W. "An Appeal for Stricter Terminology in the Textual Criticism of the Old Testament." *JSS* 21 (1976) 15–25.

Goshen-Gottstein, M. "Theory and Practice of Textual Criticism — The Text-Critical Use of the Septuagint." *Textus* 3 (1963) 130–58.

———. "The Textual Criticism of the Old Testament: Rise, Decline, Rebirth." *JBL* 102 (1983) 365–99.

Grélot, P. "Le Chapître v de Daniel dans la septante." *Semitica* 24 (1974) 45–66.

———. "L'orchestre de Daniel III, 5, 7, 10, 15." *VT* 29.1 (1979).

———. "La Septante de Daniel iv et son substrat sémitique," *RB* 81 (1974) 1–23.

———. "Soixante-dix semaines d'années." *Bib* 50 (1969) 169–86.

———. "Les versions grecques de Daniel" *Bib* 47 (1966) 381–402.

Hamm, W. *Der Septuaginta-Text des Buches Daniel nach dem Kölner Teil des Papyrus 967: Kap. I–II.* Papyrologische Texte und Abhandlungen. Bonn: R. Habelt, 1969.

——. *Der Septuaginta-Text des Buches Daniel nach dem Kölner Teil des Papyrus 967: Kap. III–IV.* Papyrologische Texte und Abhandlungen. Bonn: R. Habelt, 1977.

Hanson, R. "Paleo-Hebrew Scripts in the Hasmonean Age." *BASOR* 175 (1964) 26–42.

Hartman, L. F. and Di Lella, A. A. *The Book of Daniel.* AB 23. Garden City: Doubleday, 1978.

Hatch, E. and Redpath, H. A. *A Concordance to the Septuagint and Other Greek Versions of the Old Testament. Graz: Akademische Druck- und Verlagsanstalt,* 1954.

Jahn, G. *Das Buch Daniel nach dem Septuaginta Hergestellt.* Leipzig: Pfeiffer, 1904.

Jellicoe, S. *The Septuagint and Modern Study.* Oxford: Clarendon, 1968.

Kenyon, F. G. *The Chester Beatty Biblical Papyri.* London: Emery Walker, 1933–1941.

Klein, R. W. *Textual Criticism of the Old Testament: The Septuagint after Qumran.* Guides to Biblical Scholarship: Old Testament Series. Philadelphia: Fortress, 1973.

Kuhn, K. G. *Konkordanz zu dem Qumran-Texten.* Göttingen: Vandenhoeck & Ruprecht, 1960.

Lacocque, A. *The Book of Daniel.* Atlanta: John Knox, 1979.

de Lange, N. M. R. *Origen and the Jews.* University of Cambridge Oriental Publications 25. Cambridge: University, 1976.

Liddell, H. G. and Scott, R. *A Greek–English Lexicon.* 10th ed. Rev. H. S. Jones and R. McKenzie. Oxford: Clarendon, 1968.

Lust, J. "Daniel VII and the Septuagint," *ETL* 54 (1978) 62–69.

Mandelkern, S. *Veteris Testamenti Concordantiae Hebraicae atque Chaldaicae.* Graz: Akademische Druck-U., 1937.

McCrystall, A. "Studies in the Old Greek Translation of Daniel." Unpublished doctoral dissertation. University of Oxford, 1980.

McNamara, M. "Nabonidus and the Book of Daniel." *ITQ* 37 (1970) 131–49.

Mertens, A. *Das Buch Daniel im Lichte der Texte vom Toten Meer.* SBM 12. Würzburg: Echter, 1971.

Montgomery, J. A. *A Critical and Exegetical Commentary on the Book of Daniel.* ICC. New York: C. Scribner's Sons, 1927.

O'Connell, K. *The Theodotionic Revision of the Book of Exodus.* HSM 3. Cambridge: Harvard University, 1972.

Orlinsky, H. M. "The Septuagint as Holy Writ and the Philosophy of the Translators." *HUCA* 46 (1975) 89–114.

——. "The Textual Criticism of the Old Testament." *The Bible and the Ancient Near East,* 113–32. Ed. G. E. Wright. Garden City: Doubleday, 1961.

Pace, S. "The Stratigraphy of the Text of Daniel and the Question of Theological *Tendenz* in the Old Greek." *BIOSCS* 17 (1984) 15-35.

Rahlfs, A., ed. *Septuaginta, id est Vetus Testamentum Graece iuxta LXX Interpretes.* 2 vols. Stuttgart: Privilegierte württembergische Bibelanstalt, 1935.

Reider, J. *An Index to Aquila.* Rev. N. Turner. VTSup 12. Leiden: Brill, 1966.

Rife, J. M. "Some Translation Phenomena in the Greek Versions of Daniel." Unpublished doctoral dissertation. University of Chicago, 1931.

Roberts, B. J. *The Old Testament Text and Versions.* Cardiff: University of Wales, 1951.

Roca-Puig, R. "Daniele: Due Semifogli del codice 967." *Aegyptus* 56 (1976) 3-18.

Sanderson, J. *An Exodus Scroll from Qumran: 4QpaleoExodᵐ and the Samaritan Tradition.* HSS 30. Atlanta: Scholars, 1986.

Schmitt, A. *Stammt der sogenannte "θ'" Text bei Daniel wirklich von Theodotion?* Mitteilungen des Septuaginta—Unternehmens 9. Göttingen: Vandenhoeck & Ruprecht, 1966.

Seeligmann, I. L. *The Septuagint Version of Isaiah.* Leiden: Brill, 1948.

Shenkel, J. D. *Chronology and Recensional Development in the Greek Text of Kings.* HSM 1. Cambridge: Harvard University, 1968.

Skehan, P. W. "The Biblical Scrolls from Qumran and the Text of the Old Testament." *BA* 28 (1954) 87-100.

———. "The Divine Name at Qumran, in the Masada Scroll, and in the Septuagint." *BIOSCS* 13 (1980) 14-44.

Strugnell, J. "Notes en marge du volume V des 'Discoveries in the Judaean Desert of Jordan.'" *RevQ* 7 (1970) 163-276.

Swete, H. B. *An Introduction to the Old Testament in Greek.* 2nd ed. Cambridge: University, 1902.

Talmon, S. "Double Readings in the Masoretic Text." *Textus* 1 (1960) 144-84.

———. "Synonymous Readings in the Textual Traditions of the Old Testament." *Scripta Hierosolymitana VIII,* 335-83. Ed. C. Rabin. Jerusalem: Magnes, 1961.

———. "The Textual Study of the Bible—A New Outlook." *Qumran and the History of the Biblical Text,* 321-400. Ed. F. M. Cross and S. Talmon. Cambridge: Harvard, 1975.

Thackeray, H. St. J. *A Grammar of the Old Testament in Greek According to the Septuagint.* Cambridge: University, 1909.

———. *The Septuagint and Jewish Worship.* London: H. Milford, 1921.

Tov, E. "Three Dimensions of LXX Words." *RB* 83 (1976) 529-44.

———. *The Septuagint Translation of Jeremiah and Baruch — A Discussion of an Early Revision of Jeremiah 29-52 and Baruch 1:1-3:8.* HSM 8. Missoula: Scholars, 1976.

———. *The Text-Critical Use of the Septuagint in Biblical Research.* Jerusalem Biblical Studies 3. Jerusalem: Simor, 1981.

Ulrich, E. "Horizons of Old Testament Textual Research at the Thirtieth Anniversary of Qumran Cave 4." *CBQ* 46 (1984) 613-36.

———. "4QSamᶜ: A Fragmentary Manuscript of 2 Samuel 14-15 from the Scribe of the *Serek Hay-yaḥad* (1QS)." *BASOR* 235 (1979) 1-25.

———. *The Qumran Text of Samuel and Josephus.* HSM 19. Missoula: Scholars, 1978.

Walters, P. *The Text of the Septuagint, Its Corruptions and Their Emendation.* Ed. D. W. Gooding. London: Cambridge University, 1973.

Wikgren, A. P. "A Comparative Study of the Theodotionic and Septuagint Translations of Daniel." Unpublished doctoral dissertation. University of Chicago, 1932.

Ziegler, J., ed. *Susanna, Daniel, Bel et Draco.* Septuaginta: Vetus Testamentum Graecum Auctoritate Academiae Scientiarum Gottingensis editum 16/2. Göttingen: Vandenhoeck & Ruprecht, 1954.

INDEXES

Texts

Authors

www.ingramcontent.com/pod-product-compliance
Lightning Source LLC
Chambersburg PA
CBHW060344100426
42812CB00003B/1118